CM0082600MJ

LEGENDS UNCOVERED

The Story of Snooker Legends

Written by Jason Francis

Legends Uncovered: The Story of Snooker Legends

Copyright © 2015 Jason Francis. All rights reserved.

Foreword copyright © Jimmy White 2015

Jason Francis asserts the moral right to be identified as the author of this work.

First hardcover edition printed 2015 in the United Kingdom

A catalogue record for this book is available from the British Library.

ISBN 978-0-9575029-2-5

Published by ROK Books Limited, ROK House, Kingswood Business Park,

Holyhead Road, Albrighton, Wolverhampton WV7 3AU

For more copies of this book, please email: info@rokbooks.com

Edited by Paul Simpson

Book Design by Amazing 15

Cover by Artworks Designs

Printed in Great Britain

Acknowledgements

The publishers would like to thank Jason Francis, Jimmy White

and photographers David Muscroft, Monique Limbos and Kevin Smithers

for their unstinting support on this project

Although every precaution has been taken in the preparation of this book, the publisher and author assume no responsibility for errors or omissions. Neither is any liability assumed for damages resulting from the use of the information contained herein.

No part of this book shall be reproduced or transmitted in any form or by any means, electronic or mechanical, including photocopying, recording, or by any information retrieval system without written permission of the publisher. This book is sold subject to the condition that it shall not, by way of trade or otherwise, be lent, re-sold, hired out or otherwise circulated without the publisher's prior consent in any form of binding or cover other than that in which it is published and without a similar condition including this condition being imposed on the subsequent publisher.

DEDICATION

For Jemma, Kirbie, Ryley and Rowan – you mean the world to me!

For my Grandpa, Clifford Hocking, who first put a snooker cue
in my hand and always found a 10p for the light.

And for Michelle, you make me laugh every single day x

CONTENTS

March 2010 – Matchroom HQ

"I don't think you're going make enough money for me to fuck you over, so I'll let you do it."

Barry Hearn – new chairman of World Snooker Ltd

September 2013

"Going forward I have absolutely no problem in non-televised exhibition tournaments organised by you wherever they are staged, providing of course they do not clash with a televised event organised by World Snooker, which may prevent Tour players choosing your events over ours."

Barry Hearn

October 2014

"I think it's time we did something together. I've got an idea..."

Barry Hearn – Waldorf Hotel London

Foreword by Jimmy White MBE

I first met Jason at an exhibition in Reading; it was one of dozens I do each year, playing a few league winners and giving out the trophies. At the time I didn't know the guy I would meet would change the way exhibitions were staged for good.

He actually played me that night – not a bad player as it happens – but afterwards he told me he could get the Crucible Theatre for an exhibition with me and Alex Higgins if I fancied it. To be honest I didn't give it a thought; no one had ever had snooker there apart from the Championships since 1977. What I didn't know was that he had all these theatre contacts and had found a loophole in the contract which prevented competitive snooker with prize money being played there – but this was an exhibition.

Within a few weeks I signed up to do seventeen shows with Higgins, Cliff Thorburn and John Parrott. I also got John Virgo ("JV") on board for trick shots.

This year we will play our hundredth show, and Jason and Legends have become the main promoter of snooker in the world after Barry Hearn.

In 2012, when I wanted to stage a testimonial, there was only one man I wanted to sort it. He worked so hard to give me and my family a perfect celebration of thirty years in the game.

There's not much I do with snooker, outside of tour tournaments, that doesn't include him now. It was amazing when we got over twelve million on Eurosport for the Ryder Cup style tournament he invented. He also came up with the idea of having JV commentate live for the crowd, again something that had never been done before.

The reason Legends works is because first and foremost Jason is a fan who understands the game. All the players love playing for him, and Ronnie O'Sullivan relies on him at tournaments now for support and guidance.

You never know if a Legends show has made or lost money: he treats everyone the same whatever is happening behind the scenes – snooker needs more people like him in it that's for sure.

He may be the promoter I work with most now but he's also a mate and a friend.

CHAPTER 1

Decisions and Revelations

February 14, 2013: 11.30pm

The call came in from Los Angeles...

"I think we should do it; I've spoken to my partner and we've allocated a million dollars to make this happen."

June 2013

My mouse hovered over the email. I knew if I opened it that I was no better than them, but if I didn't, then I was denying myself the proof of knowing what I had been suspecting for some time.

It wasn't the first time I'd been copied into an email by mistake. After all, my name being Jason Francis and the Chairman of the World Professional Billiards and Snooker Association (WPBSA) being Jason Ferguson, the margin for error was always there, especially as many email programs now autosuggest the recipient after you've only typed the first letter. It's amazing the amount of sensitive information that has dropped into my inbox over the past few years!

The disappointing thing about what I suspected the content of this email would be was that I truly thought we'd got past this issue. Barry Hearn had reiterated to me on numerous occasions, both in person and via email, that he was fully supportive of the Legends Tour. In some respects I was doing a job for him by providing an income and employment for some of the retired players – players really that previous World Snooker hierarchy had dumped like over-aged racehorses who aren't good for anything anymore than the knacker's yard.

Sadly, although in many ways World Snooker nowadays *is* Barry Hearn, he inherited a few individuals from the previous incumbent who I don't think would get employed by him normally... and then of course there is Ronnie O'Sullivan, or more importantly my friendship and association with him that really gets under certain people's skins.

Don't get me wrong, there are some good people within World Snooker. Jason Ferguson is a beacon of common sense and fairness, and someone who I think becomes almost embarrassed at the behaviour of certain colleagues. I also have to say I've found the staff in Bristol incredibly efficient and friendly – then again, what I do with Legends doesn't in any way directly affect their jobs, and I would hope I am always courteous and polite in all my dealings with them. Sadly some people at the very highest echelons of World Snooker have developed issues with me and my Legends Tour... Why? Well...

If, for example, you are the commercial director, and spend most of your time in China apologising why the game's most marketable commodity hasn't travelled again to your tournaments... and then you see plans for him to appear in China at a Snooker Legends event, I can understand you being a bit pissed. After all I'm making you look silly...

Also if, for example, you are a salaried director of World Snooker Ltd but you also manage one of the top eight players in the game and are co-promoter of the approved partner to World Snooker for all German events, I guess the sight of the World Champion playing in Berlin for Snooker Legends may get your back up.... It's not for me to judge whether it's all a conflict of interests but to me, and many others, it doesn't sit right.

I don't blame Barry Hearn; he makes no apologies for who he is and what he does. Surprisingly I almost respect him for that – not that he is relying on my respect or anyone else's to make his day worthwhile. Barry is Barry, a far more successful promoter than I will ever be, and a far more ruthless man than I could ever want to be. He also knows what it's like to put his hand in his pocket and risk his own money. Ask any promoter how often they get everything right; we make money, we lose money, you just gotta hope you make more than you lose!

I didn't expect everyone to be happy with the growth or success of Legends – that's business – but I knew the 'double click' was going to end up opening far much more than a bitter email.

Snooker Legends had just achieved 12.3 million viewers on Eurosport, an event World Snooker sanctioned and supported, and Legends was now going to

Berlin with Ronnie, the current world champion, heading the bill.

The content of the email was around a plan to, and I quote, "kick out the Snooker Legends" and damage the relationship I had started with Eurosport.

Photos after the event of empty seats in the 2,500-seater Tempodrom were circulated with captions like 'Spot the crowd'. Barry wasn't involved; he's a promoter, and no decent promoter, no matter how competitive you may be, should enjoy seeing another one lose their shirt.

Everyone, including Ronnie, told me to cancel the show, to give in, to save myself 20,000 euros, but no way was I going to be bullied. It didn't matter to me if I had lost 100,000 euros, I knew my day would come. And it did, as you will read later on, the irony being that until now they won't have even realised how they did me the biggest favour ever.

You can't put a price on loyalty and friendship, or your integrity. I did the event, kept quiet, but made sure everyone in our team saw exactly what had happened.... And you know what? Sometimes if the bully upsets the apple cart, so to speak, he may find the next time he wants to buy those apples, the price goes up!

I can't imagine the last time Ronnie, Jimmy White, Michaela Tabb or Stephen Hendry all collectively refused to be paid for a show they played in – that's what being part of a team is.

The second, almost larger irony is that if I'd taken a different course following that phone call from Los Angeles in February, the announcement after my Legends Cup wouldn't have been about a one-night exhibition in Germany, it would have been about splitting the world of snooker in two.

Long before that, I'd become increasingly frustrated by the contract restrictions on players by World Snooker that scuppered plans to stage events with BTV6 and CCTV in China, featuring, of course, Ronnie O'Sullivan. At a meeting at Alexandra Palace at the 2013 Masters tournament, I challenged the board and asked them why they wouldn't allow this. I had previously requested many times to try to find a way to work together, to integrate the Legends Tour; I'd proved beyond doubt we had an audience for it and snooker fans enjoyed the nights.

The commercial director just sat there getting increasingly redder in the face, citing only that it wouldn't be in his interests to allow it to proceed – which in layman's terms meant "If you turn up in China with Ronnie you will undermine me"!

Barry wasn't at the meeting but his number two, Steve Dawson, was, and so was Jason Ferguson, although, from what I could see, he couldn't really impact what happens on the World Snooker board as he heads up the WPBSA, a separate body. Steve chaired the meeting, and the commercial director made sure I didn't get my China sanction *but* I got assurances that if I met all the sanction criteria, then any reasonable request for a future sanction wouldn't be refused. Funnily enough later that day, that same combusting commercial director received a call from the acquisitions manager at Eurosport responsible for snooker, explaining that they would like to televise my Legends Cup the weekend after the 2013 World Championships. I guess it was just coincidence!

With no clashing tournaments, and the leverage a direct request from their major broadcast partner brought, they had no option to approve it. Had they not, then perhaps I would have revisited the conversations of February 14th Valentine's night, a night I was falling out of love with snooker whilst couples were proclaiming theirs.

I had the chance to split the sport in two; it was as simple as that. The implementation of the Professional Snooker Players Federation (PSPF) would have done to World Snooker what Barry Hearn and his PDC Darts organisation did to the British Darts Organisation (BDO). No one, until now, knows how close it came.

By October 2012, Ronnie was involved. He had effectively retired: he'd not played properly since the World Championships in May and had just pulled out of the 2012 International Open, a story I will tell you later. We were in the middle of a six-date tour of the UK, and day by day the vision was becoming more of a viable proposition.

Jimmy White and Michaela Tabb were ready to jump ship. Jimmy was hardly earning from the tour anymore, and Mark Williams had committed himself if it was going to happen, although he only knew about it later than those other two. Tony Drago was also going to come with me if I did it.

More importantly, I had the secured the funding to guarantee eight global events in year one with eight professionals guaranteed £150,000 a year basic salary before any additional tournament or commercial earnings. As well as the three players who were party to these discussions, we had targeted Neil Robertson (Australia), Ding Jun Hui (China), John Higgins, Stephen Hendry (Scotland) and Alex Pagulyan. Alex would bring us Canada and was known in the USA. Four local, relevant wildcards would be chosen for each event, and we had targeted tournaments in London, Ireland, Malta, Sydney, Shanghai, Vegas and Berlin, with the World Championship in the UK year one but then moving to the home of whoever had won it for year two – thus maximising the commercial power of the defending world champion bringing the championship home to his country.

We were going to fund all travel and accommodation; events were seven days long, world champs longer; and there would be different formats for different events, so for example some with random draws each round, black ball re-spots for deciding frames for others etc.

The idea was also that the players would be commentating when not playing, to give them a new skill and some media training and experience.

The main thing we had to offer was that the eight players we eventually chose would become shareholders in the PSPF parent company and organisation. What they brought into the organisation as players now would continue to give them a revenue stream long after they had retired. I'd like to think it was quite forward thinking.

We had everything we needed, including now, of course, the funding, but it was clear to me we'd need to be sustainable as a business after year one, and of course I'd be single-handedly responsible for ripping apart the sport I loved. I was fighting with the fact that it was some of the people who were running the sport that were my problem, not the sport itself.

I was also asking Ronnie, Jimmy and others to turn their back on their association, something, almost ironically Barry and the darts players did in the blink of an eye in 1992.

I just couldn't do it, although believe me it came closer than anyone ever knew at some points.

We'd even provisionally booked a Legends event in Goffs in Ireland, under the ruse of an invitational tournament, to get the sixteen players we wanted into the Citywest Hotel to discuss the proposal and get secrecy agreements signed. It was exciting and torturous at the same time. I knew once these players committed they would never be allowed back into Barry's club, and I had serious concerns about the retributions and taking him on. Barry hasn't got where he is today without ruffling a few feathers; he's forgotten more about the sport than I will ever know, although the irony isn't lost on me that for many years the sport he now owns regarded him as their biggest nemesis.

Not one of the players we talked to worried about the sustainability of a new tour. I think the guaranteed salary probably turned their heads.

At the end of the day I decided I wanted to be known as the guy who created the Legends Tour, not the bloke who tried to split snooker in two and rob it of its most prized assets, just because a couple of people within World Snooker pissed him off...

CHAPTER 2

Into the Eye of a Hurricane

Citywest Hotel, Dublin: November 2009

It was the early flight out of Stansted, the 'red eye' Ryanair flight into Dublin. As usual the queues were horrendous; people were being made to pack and unpack their suitcases and because they were carrying one Ryvita too many they were being charged an extra £40 in excess baggage. Tempers were rising, it was a crappy cold November's morning, but I didn't care. Amid the turmoil and revolutionary atmosphere I was happy. Why? Because I was off to meet my hero.

Alex 'Hurricane' Higgins was the reason I started playing snooker. The swagger, the grace, the sheer arrogance of this man who seemed to have a blatant disregard for authority of any kind captivated a nation, including one chubby twelve-year-old boy in Cornwall, as he cried and cradled his young daughter Lauren after winning the 1982 World Snooker Championships.

Alex was different; he was box office. A genius? Well, compared to a man who performs life-saving surgery, no, but by God he could play snooker, and play it in a way the world had never seen.

Alex Higgins, and his possible participation, was the main reason I created the Snooker Legends Tour.

Alex Higgins, and the fact I sacked him after just one show, is the reason Snooker Legends is now the world's largest independent snooker promotion.

With him it was created; without him it was able to continue...

Higgins was my favourite. A bout of earache meant I missed the chance to see him play at a local leisure centre when I was eleven years old; I got his autograph though – quite ironic really.

Jimmy White was just coming on the scene and we liked him too. We hated Thorburn – God, he was so slow and based his game on stopping Alex and Jimmy expressing themselves. Cliff's game nowadays is arriving with the largest amount of luggage you've ever seen and leaving the frosting from almond croissants all over my lounge! Again I can report he is hard to beat on both fronts. The hair and moustache remain as immaculate as ever though. Kirk Stevens was someone else we all supported, whereas Steve Davis was the best, but berated on programmes like *Spitting Image* for being 'not interesting'.

I'd been warned by Jimmy White about meeting Alex, and the legendary tricks and stunts he could pull. The route to meeting Alex had to come through Jimmy, and the route to Jimmy had to go through his manager at the time, Kevin Kelly.

The first meeting with Kevin was at Epsom Golf Club, where I intended to use the booking of Jimmy for my local's leagues presentation night as a vehicle to introduce him to the idea of a Legends tour.

Kevin was late – in fact 'late' should have been his middle name. There is no doubt this man came into Jimmy's life at a time when The Whirlwind needed him. There is also no doubt that the next five to six years, and the way they lived their lives, played a part in Jimmy's decline in the rankings.

They travelled the country in an over-aged Mercedes, making a few quid here and there, playing exhibitions in anything from the finest hotels and casinos to the grubbiest of clubs, where you checked to make sure your watch was still on your wrist after shaking anyone's hand. The lovely thing about Jimmy, and you will see numerous references to this later, is that he doesn't regret a moment of it – they had a lot of fun, made a lot of money, and who needs a spare wheel or a change of clothes in the boot when that space can be taken up with a few old black and white photos that Kevin can flog for a tenner?

Jimmy had to earn money; his outgoings and commitments were huge. Five children, an ex-wife, a young girlfriend on his arm and flash cars cost money, and it wasn't coming in from tournament earnings. Jimmy and Kevin were the masters – it really was Del Boy and Rodney. The problem was the more they earned, the more they spent. I'm not judging them, and not one bit of this is Kevin's fault, but it almost cost Jimmy his job as a professional snooker player. The saviour came in the form of the Australian outback and a Geordie duo by the name of Ant and Dec. It seems as if the offer to go to Australia for a TV show, and the creation of the Legends Tour, came along at just the right time for the Whirlwind.

The first time I promised to deliver a show at the Crucible they both collectively ridiculed me – Jimmy and Kevin that is, not Ant and Dec! As Jimmy says in his own book, they thought it was a scam, and trust me, those two could spot a scam – they'd seen most of them. By the time I produced the proof of the Crucible contract, they had both agreed to become joint promoters, taking part of the business, and any profit, in return for delivering Alex.

I thought that making Jimmy a partner, and including Kevin in a share of profits, would tie them into the deal, and, more importantly, give me a buffer for the antics of Alex.

Alex listened to no one, but if anyone could get through to him on some level, it was going to be Jimmy. Jimmy travelled the country doing exhibitions with Alex. The general consensus was that Jimmy was the only person who would work with Alex – but don't be fooled. Jimmy knew having Alex on the bill guaranteed ticket sales, and large ticket sales guaranteed large merchandise sales! Jimmy has been called many things over his thirty-year career; stupid is not one of those words.

Kevin was tasked with getting Alex to sign the contract; he had met a new lady and was moving to Cork to run an organic vegetable farm. How on earth they both thought he could co-promote a Legends Tour was beyond me, especially as he seemed to have a real problem answering a phone. Then again he was hardly Alan Titchmarsh either, to be fair, more light-fingered than green-fingered.

Jimmy going into *I'm a Celebrity Get Me Out of Here* on ITV that winter meant that he would miss the UK Championships, a huge event in the snooker calendar. That decision told me two things:

1: Jimmy didn't think he could win the UK Championships

2: The money offered to live in squalor with Katie Price and cockroaches (not sure which one is worse) for a few weeks was too good to turn down.

For me it was great timing. Say what you like about these reality shows but they give the people involved a huge profile boost, and they pay well. Of course, in return, you get to eat kangaroo cock and not shower for three weeks!

I think in the end Jimmy surprised even himself, finishing third, and making some good friendships with Hollywood film star George Hamilton and chef Gino D'Acampo.

Jimmy's new girlfriend, Kelly, had travelled with him to Australia and spent three weeks in the Versace five star hotel while he shat daily in an oil drum – not a bad way to impress your new bird either, I suppose!

About this time our first shows went on sale and the news broke of a Snooker Legends Tour being created. The Crucible show sold out in about forty-eight hours – with Alex going back to play Thorburn there again, and Jimmy there as well, it was big news.

A day before I travelled to Dublin to meet Alex for the first time I delivered the news of the sell-out to all the players. Michaela was delighted, Jimmy stunned and Alex said, "Babes you should have charged double – they would have paid it for me." He was probably right!

I arrived at Citywest about 10 am, Alex was due at 11. In the days between the story breaking and this trip I'd been contacted by Jim White (no relation) from the *Telegraph* wanting to do an exclusive interview with Alex.

Within their contracts all the players have an obligation to help promote and advertise the shows at no cost to me. No chance with Alex. He wanted 1,000 Euros, the *Telegraph* offered 300, we settled on 500 – in cash of course... saves the unnecessary paperwork!

The camera crews set up; the public at the hotel were asking what was going on. News that a Hurricane was due to hit the hotel had already created quite a buzz. Jimmy told me he'd be late, I'd warned everyone. I was on edge, but Jim White was relaxed, explaining he'd interviewed George Best so he was able to handle Alex.

I was ready, I had three hundred euros in cash ready to cover any eventuality – all I needed was for this day to go smoothly, for me to weather this Hurricane.

At 11am on the dot a cab pulled up outside Citywest... It was Alex, on time.

I was prepared for the physical state he was in, I was prepared to be hit with the cab bill (and of course I was), I was prepared to stick to my guns and not pay any more money than was in the contract we had signed... What I was not prepared for, when I held my hand out to shake his, was the full kiss on the lips I got. "Hello babes... you owe me sixty euros for the cab." He put me on the back foot straight away. I was gone. Snooker's royalty had arrived in Dublin, and he was demanding that every protocol was followed.

I had brought Steve from my office with me; he was visibly shocked at this skeleton of a man in front of me. Alex was very thin, but his mind was sharp and he was holding court.

We'd arranged to go down to Palmerston House, the private residence of Citywest owner Jimmy Mansfield. We'd do a photo shoot there, as it had a snooker table, and then return to the hotel to record the interview for the *Telegraph*.

Everyone was getting photographs with Alex. I desperately wanted one too but had to try to remain cool: he already had me at a disadvantage.

Steve, Alex and I sat at a table. Alex had brought me a gift, a gift! It was a black and white photo of him from 1974 that wasn't in circulation. He said I could get them copied and we could sell them at the shows as no one would have it. I was thrilled, then of course he said, "And I only want five euros a piece for them"!

Alex wanted to talk about the tour. I asked Steve to fetch out the current tour dates and details. "No need," said Alex as he already had the full dates and venues written on three betting slips, one for May, June and July. Next to the Crucible date were the words SOLD OUT – I feared the worst.

I'd already been fleeced for a cab fare, and a first class train ticket from Belfast soon followed. He wanted to know if the *Telegraph* had brought cash for the interview, but then to my amazement started suggesting we did a show in Ulster Hall in Belfast and a venue in Blackburn he had played at.

After Alex had a pint of Guinness, with a quick rum chaser, we travelled down to Palmerston House. Alex reminded me that he needed to put our branded shirt on with the Snooker Legends logo – he wanted a private room to change in and it was just the two of us.

For five minutes the façade dropped. It wasn't easy to have any conversation with Alex as the throat cancer had ravaged his vocal cords and he could now only communicate with a quiet rasp. He was difficult to understand and obviously any speech was painful for him. I later learned it was the scarring from the chemotherapy.

I gingerly helped Alex out of his full length coat and long sleeved shirt and we put the Snooker Legends polo shirt on. I was shocked at the state of him: not so much the malnutrition, as you could see that through his clothes, but his upper body was covered in scars and what I can only guess were liver spots. He saw I was shocked and broke the silence. "Don't worry, babes, I'm still breathing." I laughed almost in embarrassment; the man who once showed unbelievable strength of character in the face of adversity now didn't have the strength to lift his arms above his head to put on a polo shirt.

Sadly even he agreed that the small size hung off him like a bin bag and his forearms were in a bad way, so we put his shirt back on to cover his arms and the polo shirt went on top – but we were kidding nobody.

Alex shuffled into the games room and a transformation took place. Almost immediately his eyes switched on, he stood up straight, and headed straight for the cue rack. "Let's have a game."

The Hurricane was back at a snooker table. The security blanket was twelve foot by six, and the shuffling soon became a swagger. The lights had to be moved: we'd only been planning to take a few shots at the table but now Alex wanted a game... and I was going to be his opponent!

The *Telegraph* crew were protesting to Jim White about the time it would take and how this wasn't in the schedule. Jim White wasn't stupid. He told them to put the normal photo cameras away and get the film cameras out – Alex Higgins playing snooker was something you didn't really see anymore.

I was a bit stunned to be honest. The table was old, the cloth threadbare and the balls resembled Edam cheeses, but was I going to turn down this chance to play him? No way.

There were four cues in the rack. Two didn't have tips; one had a tip that looked like a blueberry muffin; one tip looked pretty decent. Alex, of course took the only decent cue in the rack; after all this was going to be all about him. Tell the truth, I'd have played him with a broom handle.

I had the break-off; the camera crew were rearranging their equipment. Alex was busy banging the shaft of the cue he had chosen on his palm, apparently checking for its stiffness.

Whereas most players use maybe one or two cues throughout the whole of their careers I believe Alex had dozens. Was he always looking for perfection? Maybe, but I'm sure many had to be replaced after being broken across someone's shoulders or lost as collateral in a card game in one or more Belfast pubs.

I was shitting myself. I'm a fair player but in this situation, with this table, and a tip like a soggy marshmallow, I feared the worst. I broke off, touch of right hand side, hit the fourth red and came back inside the blue nestled perfectly frozen against the top cushion. I looked around. I'd played perhaps the perfect break-off, but was anyone looking? Not a chance. People were messing about with camera leads and lights, and Alex was still using the natural light of the window to inspect the ferrule on his cue. I'm sure I could have placed the ball there by hand and no one would have noticed.

I handed the only piece of chalk to Alex. I wouldn't see it again. He had no shot; the only red he could see was tight on the cushion just past the middle pocket. He could either clip thin off the edge of it and play what we call a 'dump shot', or come off a cushion and drop into the pack.

What he couldn't do was roll the red four feet up the cushion and drop it dead weight into the corner bag. The place went mad – of course now every fucker was watching. Alex just grinned. "Never lose it, babes," he rasped.

We played for fifteen minutes and Alex was happy to pause on shots for them to get a good camera angle. He probably made the odd twenty, nothing spectacular.

I made a couple of colours but had to pick them myself – our friendship wasn't blossoming that much! It was obvious he was lacking any cue power but the touch and feel were still there, even on this table. The lighting was very poor and the cameramen were having to supplement it to get any sort of image. It didn't bother Alex – "I grew up playing in the dark," he remarked.

At the end of the game we wanted to do some photos at the front of the house. I put my cue in the rack, Alex held onto his. "I like this cue, I'm having it," he proclaimed.

The housekeeper at Palmerston House looked a bit flustered. "I'm sorry Mr Higgins, but that's Mr Mansfield's personal cue, so I can't let it go"

The reply was genius. "Get Mr Mansfield on the phone, and tell him Mr Higgins wants his cue, and I'm not taking no for an answer."

She was unmoved, far braver than I would be. "Sorry Mr Higgins but I can't do that as Mr Mansfield is on holiday, but if you'd like to call him next week..."

She went on talking, but by that time Alex had thrown the cue on the table and headed up the stairs outside for the photo shoot. She'd won; I almost wanted to take her on tour!

Jimmy Mansfield was a pretty formidable character. According to a 2003 report, when he sold 100,000 tonnes of machinery, which had been left over from the Falklands War, the *Irish Times* estimated the profit at £19 million in the US and a further £7 million in the UK. He realized that land was going up in value in Ireland in the early 1990s, and he successfully secured several thousand acres near Saggart, County Dublin. He successfully turned this land into the Citywest Hotel and built the private residence we were currently using for the shoot. He carried on dealing in his machinery trade which once again added to his wealth, amounting to a reputed 200 million as of 21 February, 2010. But he wasn't Alex Higgins was he?

The photo shoot went relatively smoothly, mostly because the bloke was petrified and Higgins ran the show, telling him where to stand and how to take the photo.

Before we left Alex asked to use the bathroom, and while we got into our cars, and said our thanks, he popped back inside. After about five minutes I sent the *Telegraph* car on ahead back to Citywest to set up for the main interview. What on earth was Alex doing?

Our host went back through the front door to see if he was ok. Once she was out of sight, Alex appeared from round the side of the building and got in the back of the car with me. It felt like a prison break.

It was only when we got out of the gate that he opened his coat to reveal Jimmy Mansfield's cue – Alex was having it after all, but to add insult to injury he only wanted the top half, so was going to cut it in half and dispose of the butt! I'm not sure Jimmy Mansfield ever found out – sadly he passed away in January 2014 – and he may not have cared. His housekeeper was last seen searching Palmerston House for a missing Hurricane and her boss' snooker cue!

Once back at Citywest the euros were handed over and Jim White got his interview. As far as I know it's the last interview Alex ever did, and as shocking as his physical appearance was, you can see the fire still burned when he talked about snooker.

He claimed he could still have been in the top thirty-two, which was folly. The aura and arrogance were still there but physically I doubted he could have managed more than two or three frames. I was worried. In my opinion there was no way he could currently sustain an eighteen-date tour with the Legends.

Had I made a terrible mistake?

CHAPTER 3

Meeting Barry

I can't remember exactly when I first had the idea for a Legends Tour. Many people have asked me, and it would be great to create some symbolic 'light bulb' moment. However, the truth, as far as I can remember, was I'd been bored shitless watching Peter Ebdon and Graeme Dott on TV take an hour over each frame – and my children's theatre company was beginning to feel the bite of the recession. I was looking at ways to use our position and contacts with the theatres to try out another type of show.

Snooker Legends was one idea I had and recreating the Sunday night darts game show *Bullseye* was another. (I actually did *Bullseye* as well, in 2010 : it sunk faster than the imaginary speedboat they offered on it for the 101 or more in six darts!)

I didn't pick snooker out of the air as a subject for a new show. As I mentioned earlier, the game had been in my blood from a young age. I didn't actually pick up a cue until I was fourteen but I won the Cornwall Under-21 championships just three years later.

I lived in a small rural village in Cornwall called Mount Hawke, a village without a pub but with a Men's and Women's Institute. It always amazed me that I could visit the Woman's Institute at any age but wasn't allowed in the Men's until I was fourteen. The Women's Institute offered coffee mornings, whist drives and talks on gardening. The Men's Institute had a full size snooker table!

At the time Jimmy went into the Jungle with Ant and Dec (autumn 2009), the world of snooker changed. In just a matter of weeks Rodney Walker, his huge salary and six tournaments a year were gone, and the self-proclaimed messiah, who had spent most of the last ten years at loggerheads with the sport, was back. Enter Barry Hearn.

The sport was in a mess and although Barry said he had unfinished business, that was bollocks. Barry Hearn saw an opportunity to make a lot of money and acquire the sport that for so many years he had been fighting. People with far longer memories than me immediately voiced their concerns, but the truth was he was the only viable option.

The WPBSA accounts showed a cash balance of just £600,000, nowhere near enough for the world's governing body to operate globally. Jason Ferguson managed to get 24% for the WPBSA but the rest was snapped up by Barry for about a quid. The commercial rights to the game were sold for less than it takes to pay for the light to play a frame in many clubs today.

You can't blame Barry: they went begging to him and he named his terms. I'm surprised they even got a pound out of him for it. It was great business for Matchroom Sport.

Jump forward five years and you will be told there is more money in the sport than ever before, you'll be told that snooker is now being watched globally by more people than ever before. Both are true, but are you seriously telling me that snooker is now a bigger sport than it was in the 1980s?

Well I'm sorry, but the top ten players in that era were all superstars earning the equivalent of a million pounds a year. At its height Barry managed most of the top players; the problem he has now is the game's only global superstar is Ronnie O'Sullivan – and he's a loose cannon.

What Barry immediately did was give the game credibility again. He had already built the PDC Darts Tour into a money-making machine, and he wasted no time in telling the players that their holiday was over. If they wanted to be full time professional sportsmen, then they better get used to playing more than eight weeks a year. The 2010 Calendar was completely restructured, with the introduction of Twelve Player Tour Championships Events, or PTCs as they are commonly known.

I immediately had a problem, as I had eighteen Legends dates booked and on sale, and now Jimmy White would be required to play these new tournaments at the same time.

The PTCs were initially widely welcomed: they were shorter tournaments played over only three days and offered a 10k winner's prize. It gave countries that couldn't fund or stage a full ranking tournament a chance to get the top players at their venues. With a field of 128 it was dog eat dog, but what people didn't see was that by allowing the amateurs to enter these tournaments, with the chance of maybe getting that plum tie against a top pro, Barry rang the death knell for the English amateur game, and to a lesser extent the International Billiards Snooker Federation (IBSF) who still represent the only route snooker has to the Holy Grail – Olympic status.

Top amateurs trying to break through onto the tour no longer invested in grass roots amateur snooker. The cheques were made out to Barry instead, with a route to tour status now possible from their own ranking list for participation, and financial investment in those tournaments. Even now in 2015 I don't think people realise what's happened

Barry can bring more money than before, he can deliver new opportunities and new territories; however what he can't do is make the game's most marketable commodity, Ronnie, travel to play in them. That is why ranking tournaments in Wuxi, China and Australia are suffering, and why the one invitational tournament in Brazil never became more than that.

There is more money, but there are also more mouths to feed with 128 professionals. There is only one person at the top of the rankings in snooker earnings, and he doesn't even play the game anymore. Accounts will show he earned more from snooker last year than Mark Selby and Ronnie O'Sullivan combined, but then again he'd say at sixty-six years old he's worth it. You can't help but admire him.

When he took over the mess Rodney Walker left behind at World Snooker, Barry brought Brandon Parker and Pat Mooney onto the board. I don't think he had much time for either of them but what he did do was bring all the German and World Series of Snooker events under his control. Pat only lasted a year or so before getting mixed up in the John Higgins affair – Pat was John's manager – but Mr Parker is still there, proclaiming to those who will listen that he is the saviour of snooker and single-handedly delivered snooker into Germany like some modern day Christopher Columbus.

Because of the tournament clashes I had to go and meet with Barry. I think for him it was about sizing up the opposition. He had taken control of World Snooker Ltd, he had seized the German and World Series events, and he had created the PTC tour. The Legends Tour was probably the only thing in snooker he hadn't yet taken control of – but then again we hadn't yet even staged a show.

I went with Nick George, who was my fellow director at my theatre company. As we were shown into Matchroom, which I believe was once Barry's home, we both took our seats outside of his office. Barry's office door was open. Maybe that's standard, maybe it was staged but we both listened to someone getting the bollocking of their lives.

Nick and I looked at each other. It was quite intimidating and there was only one voice being heard, and it was on full volume.

Out of the office came shuffling the man I now know to have been Pat Mooney, the newly appointed World Snooker Director, and manager of top player John Higgins. He looked embarrassed as he made eye contact with us, knowing that we had heard every word. We both walked into Barry's office ready for Round 2 – *ding ding!*

A warm handshake followed and it was hard to believe the calm, softly-spoken, jovial man was the same monster who had destroyed the previous entrant to that office. I arrived with gifts – photos from the early 1980s supplied by our Legends photographer who had taken them at the Crucible at the time – and in return we got coffee. It was all very pleasant.

"So tell me about it, boys," he asked and like naïve schoolboys I ended up revealing every detail of our tour, from ticket prices to touring costs and theatre deals. The only thing I didn't divulge was the player's wages, although trust me he was angling for it. He did a job on me no doubt – it was a lesson learnt.

He asked a lot about Alex Higgins. At the time I thought he was showing compassion for Alex's well-publicised ill-health; I now think he was telling me that without Higgins to sell the tickets I'd be in trouble, and by having Higgins I was guaranteed a different sort of trouble anyway!

At the end of the meeting came the quote that forms the opening of this book, and its one I've repeated many times. He said to me: "I like it, but I don't think you're going make enough money for me to fuck you over, so I'll let you do it."

I was in shock. I hadn't come to ask permission but left there grateful for getting it – if that makes sense? I was no match for Barry that day, and I'm probably not much better at it now.

True to his word, Barry helped with the clashes, and Jimmy's qualifying matches were scheduled around the shows.

Over the past few years Barry has always made time to meet with me. At a recent meeting he acknowledged that if he hadn't come along, and snooker had continued its decline with Rodney Walker, that I would have probably cleaned up. People wanted more snooker; I was going to fill that gap but Barry came along and completely rammed it full – he took my oxygen.

When Jimmy asked me to organize his testimonial I knew that there was only one man I wanted to help and advise on it: Barry. He helped from afar, set the table prices, and used his connections to sell a few tables. I probably did ninety per cent of the work on the testimonial but in Jimmy's book he credits Barry for it.

Whenever I feel frustrated by any restriction World Snooker try to impose on me I ask a simple question: what would Barry Hearn do in my position? I have no doubt that in many ways he would carry on anyway, do his events and deal with any consequences later. Some days I wish I had his fortitude.

CHAPTER 4

The Countdown to the Crucible…

By February the Legends Tour was gaining momentum. I'd visited the Crucible to measure up for my theatre set, a deal had been done with Riley to provide my table, and I'd met with Jimmy and Alex again at a Memorabilia signing event in Coventry. Even at that event Alex had boxing legends Roberto Duran and Leon Spinks running round after him.

For a while I was brought into Alex's circle, with daily phone calls asking about venues, ticket sales – constant reminders of how lucky I was to have him, and of course demands for advances and money.

Even though it was my baby, and I had sole control, I had to create 'my boss' in order to deflect and explain why I couldn't advance any monies. Not deterred by that, Alex found other ways for me to drip feed him cash.

After the debacle of the stolen cue in Dublin, he said he needed to travel to Leeds to see a man called 'Bob' to put a new joint in it. Bob had no second name and there was no phone number forthcoming when I asked for it. Alex would need a flight into Doncaster Airport – not Leeds Bradford which would surely have been closer? – and he would need a train ticket from Doncaster to Leeds. When I suggested that perhaps it would be more convenient to fly to Leeds he told me to forget the train and he would get someone to pick him up.

I duly paid the £124 for a flight to Doncaster, only to find out later on that there was no cue man called Bob in Leeds and the only 'cue' Alex was dealing with that day was the one to the tote at Doncaster Racecourse.

While Alex was high maintenance, John Parrott was the easiest and most professional player I have ever worked with.

It's well documented that JP was not on my original list of Legends. I wanted Ray Reardon, but I am so glad we got him on board. Legends is a mix of the guys who are there to pot the balls – Jimmy, Ronnie, Hendry – and those who are there much more for entertainment and nostalgia: Dennis Taylor, Thorburn, Davis and of course JV.

JP fell into both these categories, at the time we booked him he was still playing on the tour but he was a natural entertainer – hence his nickname. He has this great ability to make anyone he talks to feel special. Nothing is too much trouble and he takes the job very seriously.

In the first year of the tour it became pretty competitive between him and Jimmy; at that time we ran a format that provided one winner each night. They probably won 85% of the nights, with Dennis picking up the rest. Cliff Thorburn didn't win a night until the end of the tour, and boy did we all party that night!

The Crucible night is always remembered and documented as being the last time Alex Higgins ever played snooker. What people don't know is that it was also the night that convinced John Parrott to retire from the tour.

When I booked him he was also working for the BBC horse racing team and was covering the Grand National at Aintree the day of our launch show. This meant a mad dash after the last race across the M62 to get to Sheffield for Legends. Our VIP reception began at 6pm.

The VIP reception was something I introduced to give the fans a chance to get up close to the players. Of course they paid a premium price, but they got a glass of champagne and a prime seat as well – plus they got to spend half an hour in the reception with the players so they could get autographs, photos etc.

The VIP hospitality experience has been well-received by all our fans. World Snooker never offered this at any events in 2010 – they do now! I also brought in autograph signings after the show so although people with standard tickets couldn't enjoy the champagne reception, if they were happy to queue after the matches, then each of them could get a handshake and autograph from every one of the Legends appearing that night. Again this has proved very popular with the fans.

JP turned up in Sheffield and had to queue to get into the car park. He later was quoted as thinking, "What the hell is going on in Sheffield tonight?" He had no idea the crowds were being caused by the Legends show, and of course Alex's return.

Cliff Thorburn landed in the UK two days before the show and stayed at a hotel close to my house in Essex. My home had a snooker room and so it was ideal for practice.

Cliff became a regular visitor to my home and when my stepson used to tell people a famous snooker star was at his house everyday I'm sure they didn't believe him. It certainly gave him a good 'show and tell' subject in his class.

Cliff is my best friend in snooker nowadays, although Jimmy comes a very close second. I had to court him a fair amount; living back in Canada he'd been out of the game for some time and was particularly bitter about having been forgotten by World Snooker. Nowadays they do stage the World Seniors Championship but I'm still not sure that's the right vehicle for these guys who graced the game and helped build it. Cliff is 67 years old, Dennis is 66 – should they really be competing against Mark Williams who is just 40 and still in the world's top twenty? There is a danger that with the current tables you make these guys look silly – that's not fair.

Dennis and Cliff have both made centuries on the Legends Tour, they've both also both beaten Ronnie O'Sullivan over single frame matches: the pockets are the same size for both players. Would they beat him over best of five, best of nine? Maybe not, but in Legends they will never be exposed to that sort of risk. Why would anyone want to diminish in any way what these guys achieved?

In March 2010 Jimmy was sharing my concerns about Alex's health. I'd been sending food parcels to Belfast, and high calorie drinks. Alex said he was feeling stronger; it was like a boxer in training camp preparing for a fight. Jimmy wanted Kevin to take him into his house for a month to build him up. There was access to a table for practice but no bookies! Kevin was reluctant; Jimmy couldn't see the problem and thought it was the least Kevin could do – then again it wasn't Jimmy who was being asked to deal with the Hurricane for a month. I'm not sure I'd have managed it. Kevin never entertained it.

On the 5th April I got the call. Alex was in hospital with pneumonia – it was bad.

Jimmy was panicking; no one could provide an update. Jimmy eventually got through to Alex's sister Anne – Alex was weak and was looking at being at least a week in hospital. Well that's it, I thought, better to get him better for the next seventeen dates even if it means we have to replace him in Sheffield.

Jimmy spoke to Ken Doherty. He was playing in the qualifiers for the world championships at the Institute of Sport that same week so was nearby. He was also a former world champion, but he wasn't Alex. No one was Alex.

On the 5th April Jimmy spoke to Jean, Alex's other sister; there was no medical improvement but there was a resolve from him to be in Sheffield. Anne and Jean were adamant, as were the medical staff: Alex was in no fit state to leave hospital, let alone get on a plane and appear in a snooker exhibition. His weight was down to six stone. I didn't know what to do. We were deflecting press enquiries, not because we were trying to be evasive, but because we simply didn't know. Looking back, was it all part of the master plan by Alex? If it was, it was a bloody good one!

At about 8pm on the 6th my phone went. 'Alex Higgins Mob' flashed up – it was the man himself. "Get me a flight tomorrow lunchtime from Belfast City into Doncaster – tell no one, it's a better story. It's gonna cost me 600 euros to bribe a doctor to get me out of here, have the cash." The phone went dead.

I was speechless.

I travelled north on the 7th with Cliff. I was still not sure Alex would make the plane but I'd booked the flight as asked, and texted him the reference number. He hadn't replied. Cliff was on edge; there was thirty years of dislike between himself and Alex, but as much as he realized how important Hurricane was for ticket sales, he was aware he travelled with more baggage than Cliff himself – and that was saying something.

The journey off the M1 into Sheffield was a welcome distraction. Cliff was sharing stories of past journeys to the championships and the fact that he was about to play once more at the home of snooker was finally sinking in. Bear in mind this guy had done a 3,500 mile air trip just for one event – he wouldn't have been doing that for a night in Lewisham, trust me! Also, if you remember, in 1983 he stayed on to play the world final against Steve Davis having just been told that his wife had miscarried their baby. Sheffield had both good and bad memories for The Grinder.

At 5pm I got the news that Alex had made the plane. Against all the odds Higgins was coming home to Sheffield.

I was in the foyer of the hotel with Cliff when he arrived. If anything he looked better than when I'd seen him in Dublin many months earlier.

Cliff and Alex made eye contact. It was tense but a respectful handshake took place... and the obligatory pint of Guinness was ordered. Far from being worried about him already requesting the 'black gold' I actually thought the iron in the stout would be beneficial to his immune system. Selfishly I had to do whatever I could to get him through the next twenty-four hours.

Alex's arrival had caused a stir. Many of the event team came out to witness the arrival of the legend, and with it his legendary reputation.

He took me to a quiet corner, more, I think, so I'd be able to hear him properly. I got the spiel about the 600 euros for the doctor's release. It was pointless arguing it but Alex had a new plan, and it was a beauty if we could make it happen.

Back in 1982, when Alex won the Championships, the iconic image is one of him holding the Joe Davis trophy in one hand and clutching his daughter Lauren in the other. The emotional scenes following his 18-15 victory over Ray Reardon where he called for his baby are some of the most replayed moments in snooker history.

Nowadays it's almost a requirement that following a victory in a major tournament the winner's children and partner are wheeled out for the 'money shot' photo with the trophy. In 1982 this was not the norm – Alex once again paved the way for the scenes you see today of Ronnie and his little ones climbing all over the table being showered in confetti, or Neil Robertson and his son Alexander.

Alex's idea was to get Lauren down to Sheffield, and recreate the photo on the same spot in the Crucible, some twenty-eight years on. He thought the tabloids would pay him £2,000 for the photo. No cut to me was mentioned but I immediately got tasked with phoning the red tops.

The *Daily Mirror* wanted it, but only for £500. Alex grabbed the phone to hurl abuse and try to settle on £1,000. The problem was his voice no longer carried the authority or caused the fear that it once did.

After an hour we'd agreed on £850 with the *Mirror*, in cash, but then Alex called off the deal after saying Lauren had to go to a job interview instead. I'm not even sure he spoke to her, or indeed that they were even speaking to each other at that time. The *Mirror* carried a snippet the next day saying the great Alex Higgins had come out of hospital and was in Sheffield for the Legends Night – I'm not sure getting a few headlines wasn't his plan all along.

I got Alex sorted with room service. I think it was a cottage pie that would be soft to digest, followed by ice cream... plus some medicinal Guinness of course.

With everything going on with Alex, Jimmy had decided not to travel till the next day. I think he knew it was going to be a circus and didn't want any part of it until the last possible moment. I later found out he was in Sheffield that night, booked into another hotel up the road. If anything I understood the need to stay away. Going back to the place that broke his heart on so many occasions was painful for him too, and he had his own demons to face without getting involved in Alex's.

My head hit the pillow, I had the Hurricane safely tucked up, but what sort of storm he was going to cause the next day was anyone's guess.

CHAPTER 5
The Crucible Theatre, Sheffield
April 8, 2010

So the day had finally come. Months of planning and preparation and now we actually had to do this show.

All the players had agreed to have a chat with the BBC during the afternoon, everyone except Alex of course! These interviews formed a series of mid-session special features during the main 2010 World Championships. It was tremendous free promotion for the brand. The feature they did on Alex involved older footage with a few shots of him playing on the night. The irony is I think the BBC would have paid him for an interview, but for once he never even asked.

As part of my notion of recreating the iconic moments from past victories, Alex had agreed to wear a bottle green shirt and come on wearing his hat – just as he had in 1982. We had arranged a photo call at 5.30pm, with the VIP reception due to start at 6. The day had flown by. It was the first time we had set up the event and we were finding our feet.

At 5pm we had finished the set-up. I was pretty proud of how it looked. We had transformed the Crucible and taken it back thirty years to the Embassy era of red carpets and gold trim. Kevin showed up in his tuxedo having done fuck all, all day. Co-promoter my arse!

Jimmy had already arrived and was having a knock on the table, soaking up the venue that had been the scene of such emotions for him. Kevin had bad news: Alex wanted his money now and he wanted an extra £500 on top.

I was fuming. He had me over a barrel and the truth is, I would have paid it.

Jimmy stepped in and said, "If you do it this time, you'll have this every time we play – tell him to fuck off and that you're calling Ken to come and replace him."

It was not his business to get involved but I think he genuinely felt sorry that Higgins was trying to screw me over. I relayed the message to Kevin who was sent scuttling back to the Jury's Inn in his evening suit to pass on the news.

Jimmy reassured me Alex would play; I had the one thing no one had ever been able to offer him since 1994: a chance to play in the Crucible. He was right.

5.30pm came and we all assembled at the table for the photo, all except Alex who was still in his dressing room. Like a lap dog I went to get him after being told he wasn't ready. I opened the door, and he was sat fully dressed with his feet up, looking at the *Racing Post* – of course he was ready, but it was their place to wait for him. The green shirt didn't fit but Alex didn't want to roll up his cuffs – once again I'd soon realize why, clever bugger.

Photos were done. Little did I know how many times that image would be used over the coming months globally.

It was April 8th 2010, and in just nine weeks Alex Higgins would be dead.

The format for the evening pitched two players into semi-finals in the first half, with John Virgo doing some trick shots and impressions. The second half would be a fun doubles with two members of the audience partnering the losing semi-finalists, before the final of the event itself to decide who would win the Legends Cup.

The initial match-ups were easy; Jimmy and John Parrott would recreate their 1991 final as a warm up to the main event, a rematch between sworn enemies Thorburn and Higgins from 1980.

The 1980s were the boom time for snooker, and remember, in 1980, TV only had three channels: Channel 4 didn't start until two years later. The nation had a limited choice of what to watch. Snooker viewing figures were massive, the top players all superstars and household names.

In the 1980 World Championships the top eight seeds didn't play in round one, Thorburn was seeded three and defeated Doug Mountjoy, Jim Wych and David Taylor to get to his second final, the first having been a 1977 loss to John Spencer.

Alex had to play from the first round and had beat Tony Meo, Perrie Mans, arch rival Steve Davis, and Kirk Stevens. It was a final between two bitter rivals but Alex thought it was destined to be his year and started showboating, playing extravagant shots; he led 9-5 overnight. Apparently that night Alex placed an order for a celebration cake, to be inscribed "Alex Higgins 1980 World Champion". Day 2 and Thorburn came out firing; he tightened up his game and clawed back the deficit.

During the final session these two gladiators went blow for blow, but unbeknown to them, a few hundred miles down the road in London hand grenades were being thrown and people's lives were being lost.

As famously reported, the coverage of the 1980 snooker final was interrupted by reports of a siege in London. The BBC took the snooker off the air to bring live coverage of the SAS storming the Iranian Embassy in Kensington. A group of six armed men had stormed it a few days earlier and taken twenty-six people hostage. The hostage-takers demanded the release of Arab prisoners from jails in Khūzestān and their own safe passage out of the United Kingdom. The British government were not going to give into their demands, and after one of the hostages was murdered, the SAS were sent in to resolve the situation.

This was a worldwide act of terrorism but as soon as the BBC switched off the snooker to start reporting it, they got bombarded by the public demanding Alex and Cliff be put back on! Can you imagine that nowadays? "Sorry, we have to leave coverage of the Twin Towers because Mark Selby and Shaun Murphy are into a decider"?

A compromise was reached, with the coverage switching between the two events. It's even been reported, although not verified as far as I know, that Margaret Thatcher had a TV set on following the snooker as well!

In 1980 Thorburn was the underdog, Higgins the people's champion. In 2010 not even the most fanatic of Alex disciples would have bet on him to beat Cliff.

What was amazing was when Alex got his moment, walking into a packed arena on the back of a huge build-up from John Virgo. Nine hundred people stood up and applauded, thanking Alex for what he had done for the game of snooker. He was back home for the first time since 1994. What followed was largely irrelevant – they had seen their man.

Alex was playing with the hybrid cue, top half Jimmy Mansfield's and bottom half from God knows where. He had cut the thumb from some bright yellow marigold gloves and stretched it over the butt of the cue to give him some sort of tactile grip – it was very bizarre.

The cuffs were now rolled up. Why? Well, because on his right wrist, in full view of the cameras was Alex's hospital admission band – he never missed a trick!

I've been criticized for allowing Alex to play. Some said the whole thing was a freak show and I was exploiting him just for ticket sales. If you had never met, or been around, Alex then maybe I could understand you having that opinion. If on the other hand you had ever had anything on any level to do with him then you would know that *no one* told Alex what to do. He checked himself out of hospital, travelled to Sheffield and played that night because he wanted to do it.

Could I have stopped him? I could have tried, but who was I to deny a man who had done so much to get to the venue the chance to play in it?

I'd mentioned to JV about not just doing the trick shots but also giving some live commentary during the frames. I was always aware that we had to set ourselves apart from tournament snooker.

We couldn't compete with the standard being dished out by O'Sullivan, Robertson and Selby, but we also didn't have the restrictions that tournament snooker brings, where one cough in the crowd on a player's backswing can cost them a title and a good few quid.

JV wasn't immediately sold on the idea but agreed to give it a go. When you have natural entertainers like Parrott, Taylor and Davis playing, then they fill in the gaps, with a joke here, and a story there.

My issue was that if Jimmy wasn't potting balls and making big breaks, or Cliff was struggling or having an off night – as they all do from time to time – then the show could become embarrassing.

JV provided the glue to hold it all together. What he did was perfect; it worked far better than I could ever imagine and has become a feature of all our Legends shows.

John Virgo knows when to speak, and more importantly knows when to keep quiet. If a frame goes messy he will be out at the table offering advice on a 'plant' or certain shots they should play. If O'Sullivan is on nine reds and nine blacks, with a maximum looming, you won't hear JV telling you about when Ray Reardon found a talking frog!

In my contracts, mainly because of Alex, I had inserted a clause banning alcohol from backstage. All these Legends, save JP, had a reputation for enjoying a small libation and I was terrified of them getting pissed and making a fool of themselves, and more importantly the event itself.

The clause was ignored; the green room fridges were filled with Budweiser and Guinness and even The Grinder Cliff was demanding "Two fingers of vodka and some tonic". (Two fingers were the measure taken from the bottom of the glass.)

The first half went well. JP defeated Jimmy, another loss for Jimmy in the Crucible, and Cliff easily defeated Alex 2-0.

During the twenty minute interval I was doing the rounds. The atmosphere was good but Jimmy was nowhere to be found... unless you were in the queue in the foyer lining up to buy his merchandise and get a signed photograph!

I was fuming. Snooker Legends had our own merchandise, including Jimmy photos he would sign, and by sitting there chatting, he was devaluing every VIP package I had sold which gave the people who paid their time with the players. You could argue why would you pay for a VIP package if one of the main stars was going to sit by his own shop in the interval? It was pure greed and detracting from the official sales.

I wasn't happy, and even though I didn't know Jimmy or Kevin that well, I let them both know it was unacceptable. It never happened again! I was struggling to make Jimmy see that this was not a two-bit exhibition in some back-arse club where you try and nick a few quid before the clientele have the wheels off your Mercedes.

It didn't take him long to buy into the Legends notion or ethos and it's one now he defends fiercely. Ironic really.

The rest of the evening went well; Michaela Tabb, the lady referee, had been a delight and was so good with the public. It still annoys me now when players are signing a piece of merchandise for a fan whilst looking the other way or having a third conversation. Jimmy can still be guilty of this whereas Michaela makes everyone she meets feel like a million dollars.

Alex remained fairly well-behaved. People queued for ages to meet him afterwards, and he shook every hand and signed every photo. The plan was to go back to the Jury's Inn for a little reception and I thought I could finally relax.

Alex was still on about his 600 for the doctor; I knew I'd have to pay it from the merchandise sales. As with all these things I got caught up at the venue for a while and didn't get back for forty-five minutes.

Higgins had gone off to bed screaming that he hadn't been paid and had been ripped off; no one else seemed to get caught up in his theatricals. I went up to the room with my colleague Nick to find a note punched across the door handle.

It started with the words "Dear Jason" but after that the pleasantries ended, and he said he felt let down and ripped off. I knocked on the door and was summoned in. Alex was in bed with what seemed like his life's possessions strewn over the bed, all within reach. "Where's my money?" he rasped.

"It's here, Alex," I said and went to give him the envelope with £600 in.

"Put it on the bed, I'll be checking it."

I welcomed him to check it and explained I had been caught up packing up, that's why I was later getting back – not that I had set a time. It dawned on me that he wasn't actually pissed off with me but he was now in a place where he could exert some authority and be an arse, so I was the focus of it.

"I want more money next time and I'm only playing Jimmy. I want the money up front and I want someone with me at all times to look after me."

I explained that Kevin was supposed to be looking after him...

"Fuck that Irish c**t – you can do it."

"Alex, you've signed a contract and agreed the money. I'm not paying you any more money, and I can't just have you playing Jimmy."

Alex pulled back the covers and swung his legs over the side of the bed. Nick later said he thought he was going to come for me. The truth is he hardly had the strength to sit up.

"You pay me more money or I'm not playing."

"Then don't play, Alex," I said, I think overcome by tiredness and emotion of the day, and of course his unreasonable behaviour.

"Fuck off out of my room," he said. "More money or I ain't playing no more."

I retreated to the door and then knew this couldn't go on.

"Alex, I need to know if you are going to play the rest of the tour. I want you to be happy but not everything can revolve around you."

The reply was genius.

"Listen you c**t, everything does revolves around me... Now fuck off!"

I pulled the door closed but then reopened it. "I'm sorry Alex, but I'm not prepared to work like this. I won't be using you on the rest of this tour."

"Fuck off!" he rasped and the *Sporting Life* was thrown in my direction, landing well short of the door but far enough from him to ensure that he was going to have to get up to retrieve it before he could place his next bet.

I returned downstairs. Nick was fully supportive, but I was in a daze. The party was in full flow, Jimmy and Cliff sharing old stories and JV into his third or fourth lager.

Michaela handed me a pint. We'd only met earlier that day but already I had a strange feeling we were to become great friends. Jimmy and JV came over for a chat.

"Brilliant night, Jay," said Jimmy.

"Superb," added in JV, "and a great idea to do the live commentary."

"We can do hundreds of these," said Jimmy. "All we gotta do is find a way to control him [meaning Alex] and get him better."

"Yeah, Alex is the key," said JV.

Little did they know I'd already sacked him, and although we'd speak again on the phone it was the last time I'd ever see the Hurricane!

CHAPTER 6

After the Hurricane...
and That Night in Blackburn.

The tour made national news and elevated Snooker Legends into the snooker public's eye, but with just one show done I already had a PR disaster on my hands. The 'top of the bill' had been sacked and no one knew.

I'd broken the news to Virgo first, who thought I was mad and begged me to phone Alex. "You know what he's like; Jimmy and I have had a lifetime of it. That's Alex."

Jimmy was more balanced... "We're still gonna get paid for the eighteen shows right?" Priorities straight as ever from The Whirlwind.

Cliff knew it was the right decision. Alex had already been such a disruptive influence that the thought of the next seventeen shows going off without there being a major incident between those two, or Alex and any of the team in general, was unrealistic. Ticket sales were going well; what was called for was a strategy of damage limitation.

I'd decided not to take JV's advice to ring Alex and got Cliff to speak with Dennis Taylor instead. Dennis was Cliff's best friend on tour and The Grinder thought Den would fit in perfectly. He was a former world champion, so no one could say he wasn't a legend, and he'd played in the most-watched snooker final in history in 1985. He was also another member of the BBC commentary team, which was key. In that first year the tour got advertised live on air during matches he was commentating on literally dozens of times; I don't think you could overestimate how valuable this was. It was certainly something we could never have funded. I got away with it for two years before the BBC clamped down on it. It was getting comical, with fans forecasting how many times Dennis would mention the Legends Tour during his broadcasts – good fella!

Dennis said he would love to join the tour but had a clash on a few of the dates so I'd need to cover them. I was still in turmoil. Interview requests were still coming in for Alex, which of course we had to politely refuse anyway, but I was aware people were buying tickets to see Alex play and I knew we were misleading them. I also knew the next morning I had to speak to the venues and issue a press release.

At about 9pm that night my phone flashed. It was Alex. "Jason it's Alex. How much was in that envelope?"

"It was £600, Alex, as agreed."

"I didn't count it but I think someone stole some of it from me."

Awkward silence.

"I'm not well, and don't think I can continue on the tour."

My head spun. What? "Just three days ago I sacked you – what are you on about?" I thought.

"Alex, I've already spoken to Dennis Taylor about doing the rest of the tour in your place."

"He won't sell you any tickets. You need me but I'm not well enough."

I knew what he was doing: I still owed him £500 for an autograph session he did for me before Sheffield so we could make up some memorabilia. The deal was he would get paid when it was sold.

"I'll let you know when I'm well enough and we'll do some more, but just me, Jimmy, and John Virgo, and the referee is ok as well."

This was a very different Alex from the one who screamed at me in Sheffield. I agreed to issue a statement saying he was not well enough to continue the tour. I wouldn't mention I sacked him and he agreed not to say anything bad about Snooker Legends... Oh and I was to send the £500 to him the next morning, first class of course.

This was the last time I would ever speak to him. We parted on ok terms and he did concede it was good to play again in Sheffield, but said his 'tip' had meant he couldn't play properly. If that is what he wanted to believe then so be it.

Pictures of him turned up in a newspaper a few weeks later in Marbella where someone had raised some money for him to get his teeth sorted. Amazingly he was wearing the same green shirt I'd given him in Sheffield: it must have been 100 degrees in the Spanish sun and here he was in long sleeves. The reality was, I think, at the time it was probably the best shirt he owned.

No one was surprised when we announced his withdrawal from the tour. Dennis was on board, and Jimmy got on the phone and sorted Ken Doherty and Mark Williams to do the dates he couldn't.

By the time we got to Telford some three weeks later everything had settled down. I was quickly losing patience with my 'co-promoter' Kevin, and also now that I didn't have to deal with Alex and had the personal contact with Jimmy, I felt that Kevin had very little left to offer the tour anymore. He earned a few quid from the Crucible date, enough to buy his poly tunnel to grow his organic veg in Cork! We never fell out, but he had no purpose on the tour any more.

At our second show the Legends Tour really took shape. It was still a night of snooker, but now we added entertainment. The tension was gone and Dennis fitted in perfectly. Jimmy seemed more relaxed, and there was no sign of his personal merchandise stall. We laughed all night.

After Telford we went to Brentwood, Llanelli, Cardiff and Hoddesdon. A great night followed at the Assembly Rooms in Derby, then on the 22nd May we arrived in Redhill, Surrey, for what was to be anything but a normal Legends night.

At the previous seven events the Legends Cup had been shared between Jimmy and John Parrott, apart from Cardiff where Mark Williams played and just made everyone looked silly with two centuries in three frames despite playing with a 'light white' ball! It was amazing how competitive they suddenly all became.

Cliff was struggling for form, adapting to the fast cloths and a tournament table again. Dennis had made his first Legends century and was playing well, but he wasn't beating JP or Jimmy. We rotated the match-ups and when Dennis faced Cliff, it was not one for the purists, that's for sure.

Redhill is in Surrey and Jimmy lives in Surrey, which meant I knew his requests for tickets might increase that night. With five kids, and more hangers than a dry cleaners, I think I could have filled the venue that night just with his entourage.

The event had sold well and quickly the ten tickets Jimmy needed became twenty, then twenty-five. We had nowhere to put them all but I was expected to just create seats. I wasn't in the best of moods, plus he turned up with his partner's family and was already well into the Budweiser by the time the VIP reception took place.

It was our seventh show in two weeks and everyone was tired. Michaela Tabb, our usual referee, was already booked elsewhere so a less-experienced referee, Trish Murphy, was stepping in.

JV did his trick shots and lifted the crowd, and JP went on to play Dennis, Dennis threw an 80 break into him and won comfortably 2-0. During this time a further six Bud bottles lay strewn backstage near where Jimmy was supposed to be waiting to play!

Jimmy was the worse for wear when he went on to play Cliff. The first frame was awful; Cliff was struggling and Jimmy was pissed – it wasn't really what people had paid for. Budweisers were appearing at the playing table, courtesy of one or more of the extended family – the mood was a little uneasy.

Jimmy took the first frame; JV was doing his best to keep everyone entertained. To say it was a struggle is an understatement. Into frame two.

After a safety exchange, Cliff missed a long shot and left Jimmy an easy red along the top rail. The Whirlwind dropped it in but was left low on the black; if he took it on he was certain to split the pack everywhere.

He smashed the black in at about 100 mph and the table looked like someone had emptied a bowl of cherries all over it. More importantly he was plum on the next red, and the black went into both pockets. Soberness descended on the Whirlwind.

By the time we got to ten reds and ten blacks you could hear a pin drop.

A maximum '147' break is a rare thing in snooker, Hendry and Ronnie hold the tournament record of eleven or twelve each I think, but that's in a career that has spanned twenty years each and hundreds of tournaments. Twelve reds, then thirteen... it was on. Here was a man, who at a conservative guess must have had ten bottles of beer in him, on course to make the first ever Legends Maximum. Trish was shaking more than Jimmy; she was closest to the action.

The fifteenth black went in. You could cut the atmosphere with a knife. Yellow, green, brown followed, tricky blue... it's in and we are on the pink. Deep screw off the side cushion on the pink, never a gimme... yes!

I didn't hear Trish say the words "147". The crowd erupted and we got a bit of a pitch invasion as everyone congratulated Jimmy. He had done it.

We sat in the dressing room in the interval and the mood was amazing. Jimmy seemed sober; collectively everyone knew that this maxi gave the tour huge credibility. This was not just old farts knocking a few balls about; they could still perform!

After the doubles match Jimmy and Dennis were introduced for the one-frame final. Jimmy screamed a long red in, took the black and once more split the pack. By the time he had taken only the fourth red and black the murmur had already started...

"There's another max on here," I thought to myself, barely able to comprehend what was happening.

Already the only problem ball I could see was the pink; it was tight to the cushion. It was weird but I had no doubt in my mind that all the remaining eleven reds were going to be taken with blacks; Jimmy was hitting the ball so sweetly. There was a real chance we could see back to back maximums. I was right and the break reached 120, just the colours for history.

Yellow, green, brown were dispatched no problem. Jimmy was going to need to use the angle on the blue to move the pink.

The blue crept in off the knuckle. It wasn't a clean contact by any means but agonisingly the cue ball slipped past the pink. The crowd groaned, JV kept the faith.

"if any man can find this, Jimmy can," whispered JV.

Jimmy's only hope was a double on the pink, it jawed and the break finished on 134 – we almost felt disappointed!

Jimmy White was two balls away from creating snooker history, back to back maximums.

I left soon after the show. I don't think they celebrated with Budweiser's: the bar was dry and the next dray delivery wasn't due till Tuesday!

The night after Redhill was a bit of an anti-climax, quite understandably, but by the time we got to King George's Hall in Blackburn on the 28th May we had another reason to celebrate: it was Dennis Taylor's birthday!

During his professional career Dennis had based himself in and around the Blackburn area. People often report his famous fall out with Alex Higgins when Alex threatened to have him 'shot'. They don't report that when Alex first came over to the UK it was Dennis who got him a flat in Blackburn and set him up with a TV set and a few quid spending money.

Alex once claimed that they fell out because Dennis fancied one of his sisters. The truth was the other way round, and Dennis has always refused to repeat what Alex said to him that caused the rift.

Dennis was the good guy from Belfast, Alex was the bad boy, and everyone loves the bad boy. Dennis didn't try to compete.

He'd created his own piece of history in 1985 when he beat Steve Davis to win the world title; to this day, that final achieved the highest ratings ever on BBC2, over eighteen million. With his trademark 'upside down' glasses he developed his own character and he was a natural performer, perfect for Legends.

All the players on the tour claimed they never practise much. Utter rubbish. I don't think Ricky Walden's table in Chester was ever busier than during Legends season. Dennis was certainly putting the hours in; he hadn't played properly for eight years before the Legends Tour, last thing I heard he was considering a little entry to the world championships! Trust me, he can still play the game.

Blackburn was a party atmosphere. As well as Dennis' family we also welcomed John Parrott's, the venue not being far from his home in Formby. Both of them were keen to impress, but they were drawn to play each other that night.

Dennis had already won a Legends night, Cliff had not, and it was bothering him. He was also the only one who hadn't yet made a century; that too was bothering him. Even at sixty-five, he was trying different approaches: one night he would practise before the game, the next night not. One night he would have vodka, the next night a coke – he was searching for whatever formula would get him a win.

JP went on against Dennis and never got a shot. We all felt for him, but Dennis made 90 in the first frame and a century in the next. The trademark wagging finger and cue above the head were on show and the crowd loved it. JP was disappointed for his family. "At least you've got the doubles," I said. "Make a few in that."

The truth was the players hated playing the doubles; it's not so bad if you've got a competition winner who plays a bit, but generally you get two random winners in the raffle and some of them have never held a cue before. Also of course there is no value in just seeing the legend clear the balls up; these winners deserve to enjoy playing on a world class table with a cue they've just won and partnering a legend.

Sadly for JP, two things were flowing freely that night: the first was Dennis's cue arm and the second was the alcohol that the first raffle winner had consumed, the guy who got to partner JP!

The guy wasn't short on confidence, or Guinness it seemed, and made a complete prat of himself. He basically ruined the frame. One minute he was grabbing Michaela, the next tapping the back of the pro's cue, a pet hate, and generally getting all cocky.

We all felt so bad for John. His family had come to watch him and he didn't get any chance to perform for them. Cliff was the other pro in the doubles and he seemed completely bemused by it all.

The final saw the 'birthday boy' take on the Whirlwind, a one-frame shoot out. Destiny had already decided that tonight's event was only going one way. Dennis made another 80 and only just missed out on his second century. He had won in front of his family – it was time to party!

Whenever we stay away the standard of hotel is always variable. If I can get a reasonable deal we'll stay somewhere really nice, if not it's a Premier Inn with a continental breakfast.

In Blackburn I'd done a deal with the Mecure, a stunning country hotel, and we settled into our own little residents' bar to celebrate the champ's birthday and Legends win. Dennis had his son there, Damian, and the mood was good.

The sandwiches and drinks arrived. There was a lot more of the drinks than sandwiches; everyone was having a good drink.

Out of nowhere JV stood up and started a singsong. Well, that was it. He took us through his repertoire of Roy Orbison and the Beatles and soon it became almost like 'spin the bottle' when the next person had to get up and start a number then we all joined in.

We were all slaughtered come 2am. Cliff and Dennis had performed 'Up on the Roof' by the Drifters and even I'd had to belt out a bit of Elton John.

The few other residents in the hotel didn't really know what had hit them; one particular hippy couple were especially totally confused by it all, not having a clue who any of these guys were. It was like a remake of the film *Cocoon* in there with the old boys jiving.

I don't remember what time we got to bed, all I know was it was light outside and I wasn't the last to go.

Cliff was booked to appear at a Memorabilia fayre the next day to sign autographs with Ray Reardon... in Milton Keynes.

We'd agreed to get on the road at 8am. My partner at the time was driving – she stopped drinking way earlier. I was hanging bad and as for Cliff... well, it wasn't pretty.

The trip south was about two hours but Cliff hadn't even showered. About twenty minutes outside the MK Bowl we pulled into a service station and Cliff threw some cold water over his face and brushed the moustache. He called the promoter to say he was going to be late and we'd had traffic. That would have been ok if the promoter themselves hadn't come down exactly the same road only an hour earlier!

With a packet of extra strong mints Cliff started work. Ray of course had arrived early and was looking immaculate, despite his seventy-nine years! Cliff felt really embarrassed.

I used the opportunity to try and 'tap up' Ray to guest at our Plymouth Show in July. He was one legend I desperately wanted to work with, but Ray was not over-keen.

I left Cliff and the six-times world champion surrounded by Klingons, Trekkies and some bloke from the *Twilight* film. We were off to Ireland in a few days and I needed a break, and some Alka-Seltzer!

On the morning of the flights to Ireland I got a call to say JV had been taken ill. It was another panic. Luckily Ken Doherty was able to cover the two shows and Dennis took over the commentary job and trick shots.

Killarney was disappointing sales-wise but Citywest in Dublin did well. It was on the flight between Kerry and Dublin that I first had the idea of the Legends Cup. I'd visited the K Club and Belfry as a fan to watch golf's Ryder Cup and I thought something in snooker could work the same way.

By now JP, Dennis and Cliff had become a firm unit. They ate together, played golf together and laughed a lot. I mean, a lot. Both Dennis and Cliff are hilarious in their own ways and JP laughs at anything. It was lovely seeing them have so much fun together. Jimmy always kept himself a little bit separate from them, sticking mostly with JV.

I'd noticed that JV's neck injury was becoming a problem He wasn't able to straighten his head, so he couldn't get down over the cue to play a shot.

One regret I have is that JV has never been well enough to play at a Legends event because I have never met a man who loves the game of snooker more than John. Because he has been the lead commentator for so long with the BBC, people forget just how good a player he was, winning the UK Championship and reaching the semi-final of the World's. In his amateur days I'm also told he was a fearsome money match player in the Salford area, as was Patsy Fagan.

On 15th July 2010 it finally happened – Cliff won! He beat Jimmy in the final. It was a huge relief for him and boy, did he lap it up. Everyone was delighted for him and all the event girls wore the Cliff range T-shirt in the hotel afterwards posing for photos like they were his Charlie's Angels.

The tour finished in Doncaster. There was general sadness that it was over but for once it was their turn to surprise me. Unbeknown to me they had smuggled my own cue up and when we came to announce the doubles match John Virgo announced that I was partnering Cliff. I truly had no idea.

I was still in shock when Michaela presented me with my cue; it was my turn to play in front of a Legends crowd. I think Cliff broke and the other raffle winner played a shot, I got in and made about a dozen I think. JV was giving me some stick and even Jimmy was out watching. I played a safety and JP screamed one in. He made a century and I never got another shot – that's snooker for you! It was a tremendous gesture by the team and they also presented me with a signed photo from them all.

Without discussing it with the players I announced over the microphone that we'd be doing a 2011 tour. I had no doubt we were all in this for the long term.

CHAPTER 7

Booking Ray and Losing Alex.

July 10th, 2010 is another important date in Legends history. We were in Plymouth and Michaela announced words I'd been waiting a long time to hear. "The first frame, Ray Reardon to break."

'Dracula', as he is affectionately known, was always on my original list of legends for the first tour. Ray was very rarely seen anymore, only occasionally popping up at the final of the World's as a sponsor's guest. I'd tracked him down via Churlston Golf Club in Brixham, Devon, where he was the President.

He did contact me initially but felt that touring the country for eighteen nights was too much at his age. However, he did eventually agree to be the special guest at our show at the Plymouth Pavilions after I met him in person with Cliff in Milton Keynes. The original date had to be moved because of a clash with a qualifier Jimmy had. "No problem to me," said Ray. "I'm retired."

He turned up at about 3pm, just the three hours early! He wanted to get used to the table. Two of his closest friends had driven him down. They told me that he was still making centuries in practice on the table at their golf club; they too were delighted to see him honoured in this way.

Jimmy, Cliff and the boys were generally excited and a little bit humbled to have Ray there – it was like the Godfather of the sport had arrived.

Ray was a different generation to the rest of the players on the tour. Only Cliff and Dennis were playing when he was at his peak winning his titles – and they were just starting out.

Ray was from the coal mining community of Tredegar in Wales. Wanting to play snooker, he turned down a place at grammar school to become a miner at just fourteen, following in the footsteps of his father. After a rockfall, in which he was buried for three hours, he quit mining and became a police officer when his family moved to Stoke.

He won his first world title in 1970, the year I was born, beating John Pullman in the final 37-33; yes, the final was the best of 73, not 35 as it is today. It was played not at the Crucible in Sheffield but at London's Victoria Hall.

Between 1973 and 1976, Ray played seventeen World Championship matches without defeat and won the title four years in a row. When the snooker world rankings were introduced in 1976, Ray was the first number one, retaining that position until 1981/1982. His sixth, and final, world title came in 1978 when he beat South African Perrie Mans, his only victory at the Crucible. Amazingly though in 1982, despite being forty-nine, he was still world number 1. He remains the oldest player, at fifty, ever to win a ranking tournament.

Everyone talks about the 1985 final when Dennis Taylor potted the final black to beat Steve Davis in front of 18.2 million viewers. People forget that the person the Nugget beat in the semi-finals that year was Ray, who was fifty-two years old. I can't see anyone in the modern day game getting close to repeating that feat.

Back to Plymouth, and it was time to get underway.

JV would always do some impressions at the start of the show. Ray wasn't due to appear until later but we hatched a plan where tonight JV would do his 'Reardon' impression and pretend that Ray wouldn't know he was doing it, telling the audience he was in the dressing room.

We rigged a special light by the curtain and just as JV was doing the famous 'Reardon Shoulder Shake', the man himself popped his head round the curtain. It was staged but the audience didn't know that, and I don't think they cared. The place went mad.

The amazing thing about the people who attend these Legends nights is that they are all there for a reason. This is not the sort of event that's a tag-along, where reluctant relations feel they have to go – these are all snooker fans who are genuinely thrilled to see their heroes from yesteryear. I think Ray was shocked at the reception he got as well. The smile was beaming, even if the new shoes he had purchased to wear were pinching a little!

He played remarkably well, made quite a few decent balls and laughed a lot. The legends who weren't playing that frame usually stayed in the dressing room but they all came out to watch him. Here was a Legendary Legend, if there is such a thing.

While the boys enjoyed a beer Ray refused to have anything but tea until after the job was done. Finally, when we did the autographs, Jimmy got the first gin and tonic into him, and it was lovely to see him relax. I know Michaela especially loved having him around. I only wish he was twenty years younger as I know he would have been so well received on the Legends Tour.

On 10th July 2010 Ray Reardon played at Snooker Legends; on the same night, Alex Higgins died alone in his Belfast flat. It would be over a week until someone found him, a complete tragedy.

I hadn't spoken to Alex since the middle of April; Jimmy had also had very little contact, save an appearance at an event in Manchester to raise money for his new teeth. I'd seen from the newspapers that he'd been in Marbella but as the tour finished on the 17th July we all went our separate ways, and Jimmy headed off to Thailand for the 6 Reds World Championship.

I got a tip off on the 24th July from a radio presenter at BBC Belfast who I'd worked with a while back. The story was about to break that Alex Higgins had been found dead and they wanted to speak with Jimmy. I was the only contact they had. I begged them to give me some time to contact him. The last thing I wanted to do was let Jimmy hear it on a TV in some bar or restaurant in Pattaya.

I felt numb. When someone passes and you've been a part of their lives for such a short time it's difficult to know what sort of emotion you should experience. Alex wasn't my friend; he was someone I'd worked with. In early 2010 I was someone he trusted for a while, but in fact I was the meal ticket for a few months, I know that. If I am honest, he treated me very badly, but I still had a duty to let those who were closest to him know that he had passed on. Plus of course he was still my playing hero and he was gone.

I phoned Jimmy. It went to answerphone. I asked him to call me urgently.

Then I called Ken. Ken had done a lot for Alex, including staging a sell-out show in 1997 at the Waterfront in Belfast to raise money for Alex shortly after Ken became World Champion. He was with Joe Swail, another player, in Thailand. I asked if he was with Jimmy; he wasn't. I told him Alex was gone. He didn't show much emotion, stunned I think.

"Ok," he said, his voice hushed. "We need to find Jimmy."

I explained that the story was soon going to be all over the news so we didn't have long. With the media nowadays, news goes worldwide in a matter of minutes. The death of the Hurricane Alex Higgins was big news.

At that moment my phone bleeped. Jimmy was ringing back. I took the call.

"Go on son," he said. That was how Jimmy always answered the phone. I asked where he was; he was walking back to his hotel from a restaurant. I asked if he was alone; he said he was. I took a deep breath.

"Sorry mate, Alex has died."

"When?" he replied.

"I just got a tip off from the BBC in Belfast. The news is about to break but I wanted to make sure you knew first."

"Ok," he said. "Yeah, terrible news."

Then, as he reports in his own book, Jimmy went on to talk about the match he had played that day. He was talking about a new shorter cue action he'd been trying, and we discussed how happy he was with his tip.

In some ways it may have seemed totally inappropriate to be chatting about his cue action at a time like this, but this is how Jimmy was digesting the news that his best friend in snooker, his inspiration, and his kindred soul, was gone.

I said I'd spoken to Ken and I'd let the rest of the boys know. I was worried about Jimmy: I knew there would be media requests, and they'd all be looking to speak with him.

"Take care of yourself," I said.

After the call Jimmy sat on the pavement and cried for thirty minutes... alone. He cut short his plans and travelled back to the UK.

I had to deliver the news to Dennis, Cliff and JP. By the time I got to Virgo, he already knew.

Aside from Jimmy, JV was Alex's best friend in the sport. Bear in mind that during some of that time John was on the board of the WPBSA, the very body that was having to deal with the unruly Higgins. Their friendship prevailed despite all those fines and suspensions.

John would tell stories about Alex, like the time when they visited India for a tournament in 1979 and Alex, drunk, caused a huge diplomatic incident by groping a dignitary. Such was the seriousness of his actions that the players were told that they would not be allowed to leave the country until Alex had written an apology. Alex duly delivered the apology... written on toilet paper!

Alex got away with it; he always got away with it.

The truth is he affected the lives of so many people and yet in the latter years so many of those people turned their back on him. Cliff once said Alex could cause an argument with himself in a lift – I knew what he meant.

My own opinion, for what it's worth, is that Alex was angry and bitter for the way the people within World Snooker had treated him and he carried that anger, and took it out, on people twenty years on who really didn't deserve it. So many people tried to help him but he fucked them all off.

No one will ever question Alex's ability, and what he did for snooker – plus he beat cancer. Don't forget or underestimate that.

Back in the 1980s World Snooker couldn't control their most prized commodity; I'd say that with Ronnie O'Sullivan, modern day snooker has a similar quandary.

In 1980 Alex was still able to charge twice as much as Cliff Thorburn for an exhibition, the man who had just been crowned World Champion by beating him.

There is no doubt the people within World Snooker could have helped him more. They made an example of him to try and control him. If two players got fined for the same offence, and one of those players was Alex, then the Hurricane always got hit harder.

When Jimmy is asked about Alex he says he is angry, angry that Alex wouldn't help himself. But also this is the twenty-first century; should someone of his stature be allowed to die of malnutrition?

In the ITV4 life story that was done on Jimmy in 2013 he called it a "fucking liberty" – it's difficult to argue.

I didn't travel to Belfast for Alex's funeral; I felt it would have been fake. I'd known him personally for no more than six months. It was time for Jimmy, Alex's family, and players like Ken to say their farewells.

I felt almost embarrassed when a guy called Will Robinson came out of the woodwork and started doing interviews and getting involved with organizing the funeral, speaking as if he was his best friend.

I know from Jimmy that Alex didn't initially remember who Will was; he had to be reminded that Will had done some driving for him twenty years before. Suddenly Will had Alex's great niece, also called Alex, in a recording studio cutting a record and promoting it around the Hurricane's name. It all felt a bit unsavoury. He popped up again in the documentary the BBC did: while legends like Reardon, Davis, Ronnie, Barry and of course Jimmy were paying their tributes, so was Will. People were asking, "Who's this fella?"

Will did organize the Chinese meal in Manchester to raise money for Alex to get his teeth done. Jimmy went, and so did JV and Tony Knowles. It was billed as a night to raise money for a sporting hero who had fallen on hard times. As guests who had paid good money for this dinner queued to get into the restaurant they saw Alex leaving the bookies opposite having got his bets on for the evening races!

The Snooker Legends Tour organized a floral tribute; it was in the shape of a triangle of fifteen red roses. Some of the Legends from our tour were meant to pitch in; it was about £300. I paid it up front and no one ever gave me a penny towards it.

On the day of the funeral itself I was in Spain on a family holiday. I was thrilled the people of Belfast came out on the streets to show their appreciation. His coffin was carried in a horse-drawn carriage. Ken joked that Alex had probably backed one of them in the past.

In 2011 the Legends Tour came to Belfast and we did it as an 'Alex Higgins Tribute Night'. I gave his sisters about fifty tickets and asked Jean and Anne, his sisters to present the trophy.

Ken was playing, as was Jimmy. We cut together a montage of old photos and footage and put them with a song that had been written by a fan called Joe McNally. It was very touching and it was good to meet Jean and Anne.

It was sad when I spoke with Jean just after the show and she told me that there were still funeral costs left outstanding to pay. At the time of Alex's death everyone came out the woodwork and got 'busy'. People who hardly knew him claimed to be as close as family.

Closing the streets of Belfast and horse drawn carriages don't come cheap, but when it came to picking up the tab those so called 'friends' had moved on.

People always say you should never meet your heroes – I do know what they mean but I don't regret meeting Alex, and I'm proud that Snooker Legends gave him one final chance to go back and play in the Crucible.

CHAPTER 8

'The Man in the White Suit'

The 2011 tour kicked off in Guernsey and instead of eighteen dates I'd booked twenty-eight. We had some momentum going and I wanted to capitalize on it. We were adding nineteen new venues and revisiting the ones we had done good business at the previous year.

The main squad of players was going to be the same – Jimmy JP, Cliff and Dennis – with JV and Michaela, but after the success of having Ray guest in Plymouth I decided that we should try to bring in some more legends for one-off events. My guest for the Crucible date in April was one that no one saw coming – 'The Man in the White Suit' was returning.

When people review historic moments in snooker they are usually taken from the finals of tournaments, or one-off moments like Ronnie's maximum in five minutes twenty seconds against Postman Mick Price. There are, however, two matches that buck this trend and always get brought up amongst snooker fans when such discussions take place.

I don't think anyone would argue that the most famous match that wasn't a final was the 1982 World Championship semi-final between Alex and Jimmy.

A young, unseeded Jimmy led 15-14, on the brink of his first world final. With just one frame required to beat his hero he got in first and was 59 points ahead. With balls all over the table a clearance seemed unlikely, if not impossible. History shows that Alex made the finest 69 clearance the game has ever seen. He was hardly ever in prime position and just kept pulling out recovery pots under the intense pressure of knowing that one miss would hand the match to

Jimmy. Alex not only defied logic to clear the balls but won the deciding frame to take the match 16-15. He consoled his young 'apprentice' in his arms, amidst his own muted celebrations.

The other match purists point to, and one that gets replayed a lot, is the 1984 Masters semi-final, between Jimmy and the man I'd just booked to come back for the 2011 Crucible Show, Canada's Kirk Stevens.

Kirk epitomised everything that was good and bad about 1980s snooker. He had the rock star looks, a host of celebrity friends, beautiful women hanging off each arm... and a severe crack cocaine habit that almost killed him.

When modern day players complain about having to travel overseas to China for three weeks, Cliff Thorburn is quick to point out that in the 1980s Kirk, Bill Werbeniuk and he himself had to move their entire lives to the UK to play professional snooker. Those guys, and players like Eddie Charlton, were lucky if they got to spend three weeks at home a year. No one made special provisions for them.

Cliff handled it best of all; Bill turned to drink, often having five or six pints before a match to 'settle him down'. As for Kirk, he was the youngest of the players, miles from home and thrown into the celebrity spotlight when snooker was at its peak. There are urban myths about parties thrown by the late Freddie Mercury of rock band Queen where dwarves carried the cocaine in on silver platters. It was no myth: Kirk was a guest on many of these nights – sleep and rest were overrated, and the 'high' from using cocaine meant he could stay up for days on end.

I knew trying to get Kirk was a risk. He was two years into his latest effort to keep clean, and although it was working, travelling away from the trusted support network that had got him this far could jeopardize all that.

It took him a long time to agree to appear. Like any addict, part of his recovery programme was not being rushed into making quick decisions. He'd already turned down an invite to the first World Seniors Tournament because he didn't feel ready to face being away from his treatment plan.

It was a big deal for him, travelling overseas for the first time again, and facing the demons that playing snooker and especially playing snooker back in Sheffield, could bring. Then of course there was Jimmy, his lifelong friend but someone he had been in the very darkest of places with. At points in their playing careers Kirk and Jimmy were crack cocaine addicts. And what was worse was they were earning enough money to fund the addiction. For Jimmy it was more of a phase – a blow-out that started after losing to Davis in the 1984 World Final. Sadly for Kirk it became a way of life, and one that offered him an escape from his loneliness.

In his own book, *Second Wind*, Jimmy has admitted that at the time they played their most famous match at the Masters in Wembley in 1984 they were both using cocaine in between tournaments. They had film star lifestyles and while commercially for snooker they were great, this wasn't a film script. They were living it for real. Snooker was at its peak: during that 1984 match Hollywood superstar Donald Sutherland visited Wembley. He arrived just at the start of the frame where Kirk made the 147, he left straight after the final black. He later commented that he'd only ever seen one frame of snooker and Kirk Stevens in a white suit had shot the 'perfect' game. He'd seen everything he needed in the space of fifteen minutes!

Amazingly, Kirk Stevens never failed a drugs test and was never disciplined in any way by the WPBSA for substance abuse. It was only after a claim by fellow player Silvino Francisco that Kirk himself owned up to his drugs problems. Francisco accused him of taking stimulants during the final of the 1985 Dulux British Open; Francisco was subsequently fined by the World Snooker Association for the comments. Silvino had already won the match and the title, so his motive for accusing Kirk was puzzling.

In 1997, Silvino Francisco was arrested for smuggling cannabis, and served three years in prison; out of the two it's the South African who has the drugs conviction, not Kirk. Some may say that's karma. Others could say that without the accusation being made and subsequent admission from Kirk, he might never had got help.

Cliff Thorburn always said a 'clean' Kirk Stevens was a good enough player to win the World Championships. Sadly, being clean at that time was a far bigger challenge than surviving seventeen days in Sheffield. He struggled on and off the table until the 1993 season but then retired from the tour to go home for treatment. Far from not playing though, Kirk won the Canadian Open Championship in 1997, 1998, 2000, 2002, and 2008 – so I knew if we got him to a Legends he would still be able to hold a cue.

I can't over-emphasize the part Cliff played in getting Kirk to agree to the shows and travel to the UK. He was with me when we met Kirk at Heathrow, and although they were both on edge, we travelled up to Sheffield all together and having Cliff in the car helped calm and reassure Kirk.

Their friendship spanned forty years. Kirk had first played Cliff when he was just twelve years old. In those days, in Toronto, you could play Cliff for whatever money you wanted. Kirk took two dollars from his hockey bag and took on the man who in his words was "even then one of the best players in the world". Cliff recalls playing him and trying not to take the money; Kirk insisted he took it. Cliff says it's probably the dirtiest money he's ever made!

We arranged a practice session at the Star Academy in Sheffield. China's number 1 player Ding Jun Hui was there when we arrived. Although his English is not great I don't think he had any idea who Kirk was when he shook his hand.

Kirk wanted to see Jimmy; it had been ten years at least. I didn't think Jimmy was arriving until the morning of the show – wrong again! Jimmy was already in Sheffield, on his own schedule as usual.

It was a weird build-up. Kirk was on edge about seeing Jimmy again, and Jimmy was worried about seeing Kirk. Goodness knows how close these two had taken each other to death through their use of crack cocaine; I guess it bonds you infinitely.

Fate stepped in and solved the anxiety for both men.

As we were checking into the hotel Jimmy emerged from the lift, so they basically bumped into each other. They hugged and both cried; I joked later that it was like a scene from *Brokeback Mountain*! I think for those ten seconds the last thirty years flashed through their minds: here were two fifty-year-old men almost celebrating the fact that, despite every attempt to kill themselves and each other with drink and drugs, they had somehow survived. It felt like the reunion deserved to be somewhere better than a hotel reception.

Jimmy still lived in a world where he could have a drink. That was a place Kirk could not go, and Jimmy had already suggested to everyone on the team that we shouldn't drink around him.

Just as I'd put Higgins back in a green shirt I was determined to get Kirk back in the white suit he was famous for. There was no way he was going to allow me to put him in white trousers, but he did concede that the white waistcoat would be a nice touch; he also wore a lounge tie, again very 'afternoon session 1980s'. (The 2013 Champion of Champions Invitational Event brought back the wearing of lounge ties; I think it worked, although it split opinion with some of the modern day players.)

The BBC were all over the fact that Kirk was back at the Crucible for Legends; it made for a perfect feature for the 2011 Championships. We recorded the piece in the hotel in the afternoon of the event and Kirk really opened up. It was quite emotional.

Talking about his addiction he claimed: "I'm grateful for every day that I'm sober; this is just another gift of sobriety for me. I'm back here playing snooker at the Crucible. I'm free, I feel that I'm free today, finally."

Coming back to the Crucible was something he thought would never happen. Looking back, he claims doing it was part of an important step of his recovery. For many years snooker was associated with drinking, drugs and despair. In Kirk's world they were grouped together and you could not have one without the other. He had slowly broken that chain, and here he was back at the home of snooker playing snooker without the other vices needed. He was indeed 'free'.

Kirk was going to play Jimmy that night. He got a great reception and actually took the opening frame from the Whirlwind.

I'm not sure how much serious snooker was going on, but Michaela had chalked off officiating another legend, and another important step in the recovery of Kirk Stevens, Sober Snooker Player, had taken place.

We still keep in touch and I'd like to think Snooker Legends played a small part in his recovery and connected him again with the sport that made and broke him.

At the point of writing this book Kirk remains 'free' but every day remains a battle. I wish him well.

CHAPTER 9

PC David Rathband and Procuring a Nugget

Kirk Stevens wasn't the only special guest that night in Sheffield. In 2010, Northumbria Police Force were deployed to apprehend Raoul Moat, a thirty-seven year old man from Newcastle upon Tyne who was on the run after shooting three people in two days. His victims were ex-girlfriend Samantha Stobbart, her new partner Chris Brown, and PC David Rathband.

David remained in hospital for nearly three weeks and was permanently blinded from gunshot wounds fired into his police car. Moat remained on the run for days; the man hunt was national news, as was the recovery of his only surviving victim – a policeman who just happened to be in the wrong place at the wrong time doing his job trying to protect us.

In Feb 2011 I took a call from Northumbria Police. David was a snooker fan and wanted to know about attending our event at the Crucible.

I didn't want to ask the obvious question about not being able to see but the guy who called, a fellow police officer called Serge, explained David would enjoy the atmosphere of the venue and also he would communicate the action in his ear.

I had no hesitation in arranging complimentary tickets for David and Serge; he was a hero in my eyes. I spoke with David himself before the event: he called to thank me for arranging the tickets and to get details of the hotel we were staying at. He had a good knowledge of snooker and had enjoyed playing before the accident. He had always wanted to visit the Crucible.

During 2011 we had started introducing an auction of memorabilia at the events. I was never entirely comfortable with the concept, but we brought the items initially from a shop that Jimmy had a share in and all the players would get their food and drink covered from the money we made on the take. The more we made, the better the pizza we had after – that's how it worked.

On the Crucible night Jimmy suggested we took it a stage further and raffled a frame off to play against him. It all felt a bit 'market stall' to me but he convinced me we could get someone to part with a grand, and we were on 50/50 of course! Typical Jimmy.

A few celebrities were in the audience that night. I'd just started doing the short-lived *Bullseye* darts tour and former world champions John Lowe and Bob Anderson had come along, as had former snooker player Tony Knowles and Nottingham Forest football legend John McGovern.

The bidding got to about £300 and stalled. It was a flop really, nowhere near the £1,000 we thought we'd get. JV was doing his best to drive it, to build it up as a one off chance to play in the Crucible against the Whirlwind. Another celebrity from the quiz show *Eggheads*, CJ De Mooi, jumped in with £350; CJ is a keen snooker player and is seen at a few tournaments.

From the back of the Crucible by the curtains my eyesight wasn't good enough to see exactly who was left bidding but it was John Parrott who told me that David Rathband had started bidding. This was uncomfortable.

People stopped bidding and David won the chance to play Jimmy for £500. I had that sick feeling, and any colour Jimmy had in his face drained too. If we weren't careful this could turn into a very poor joke. I'd just charged a blind national hero £500 to play a frame of snooker in the Crucible.

David was helped into the arena; you could just feel that everyone was on edge. JV took control and David broke the ice himself by cracking a gag about playing a 'blinding shot'. Everyone relaxed and laughed with him, no one relaxing more than me.

JV lined him up for every shot, he made a few balls and the audience went wild. There is no doubt that John Virgo saved my arse that night.

We never auctioned a frame again and the whole auction of memorabilia at events soon disappeared as well. And of course we never took the £500 from David, despite him offering it twice.

After the event I spent about ten minutes talking with David, and we shared the breakfast table the next morning. He was so upbeat and positive and interested in what I was doing, and how the tour was going. I was fascinated by the way he was able to navigate his way round a full English breakfast despite not being able to see what he was eating.

He particularly liked Michaela; she made a fuss of him. He also insisted on buying us a drink. As one final gesture Jimmy gave him the Snooker Legends trophy to keep as a memory of his night playing him – he was one very unique man who I thought would go on to be a real inspiration for others.

On 29th February 2012, only ten months after this night, saddled with depression, David sadly took his own life. It affected us all.

It was my privilege to meet him. Rest in peace, David. I hope you're enjoying a game or two up there in heaven.

There was one glaring omission from the list of legends I'd used so far, the Nugget Steve Davis.

I'd never approached Steve because he was Barry's man, and at the time I didn't think the success of the tour was being well-received within Matchroom Sport. For some reason I never thought he'd agree to play at Legends as it would be seen as being disloyal to Barry. I needn't have worried. He said yes to appear at a night in Stoke against Dennis immediately.

I billed it as a '1985 World Final rematch' with Dennis playing Steve, and John Virgo doing the commentary. It was Saturday 14th May, the day of the 2011 FA Cup Final, which normally wouldn't have been a problem. But when I agreed this date six months earlier who would have bet on Stoke City reaching the Cup Final? They'd never made the final before, and they'd last reached a semi-final back in 1972! Typical, fucking typical.

The town was deserted; all the sports fans had made a pilgrimage down the M1 to Wembley to see Stoke play Manchester City. Eighty-eight thousand packed the new stadium, less than four hundred came to watch us.

Sometimes as a promoter you deserve to get caught out. I wouldn't have dreamed of putting on a show in Manchester, Liverpool or near Chelsea on Cup Final Day, but Stoke? Come on, you have to agree that was bad luck!

The night itself went well. Steve was new to Legends but a master of working a crowd at exhibitions, and of course with Dennis they already had a 'script' they had perfected over many of these type of shows.

If anything, I had too many entertainers on the bill. With Steve, Dennis and JV telling jokes the snooker sometimes got lost, but it still went down to the final black of course.

I never ever stage a Legends result. It's important that the public know they are seeing players going out there wanting to win as badly as if they were playing for the world title. I didn't fix this result but Steve and Dennis found it difficult to break away from what they usually do. No one complained and I can't even remember who potted the final black. It was probably Dennis; history dictates it usually is!

That was the only show Steve did in 2011, but by 2012 he became a permanent fixture on the tour, and of course in 2013 he had his own little stint in the Australian outback which brought him to a new audience, much like it had with Jimmy.

Again like Jimmy, I can't see Steve retiring in the near future. He recently said after losing to Ricky Walden at the 2014 UK Championships that he will eventually "peter out like a firework".

Steve has other interests outside of snooker and that is where he will be able to fill the gap when he does retire from the main tour. That's a luxury Jimmy doesn't have.

As long as he is willing and able to hold a cue I'll always use him... After all, it's never bad to have a six times world champion on the bill is it?

CHAPTER 10

Meeting Ronnie

When I started the Legends Tour it was not for people like Ronnie O'Sullivan, but when the game's only global superstar wants to join the team and play in some shows, then it would have been commercial suicide to have turned him down.

I have always been respectful to the older legends like Cliff Thorburn and Dennis Taylor, so you will never see a show staged with Ronnie playing just either of them. It wouldn't work on any level and I wouldn't want to put either of those former world champions through it.

Ronnie hates exhibitions, fact. Before we came along, the term 'exhibition' to him meant grotty clubs, drunken people, and the pressure of making a maximum 147 break every frame, on substandard tables with crap balls. It was a no-win situation in his eyes and he admires how Jimmy is able to do it night after night.

At Legends we try to recreate, as best we possibly can, tournament conditions. I am anal about the organisation: everything has to run like clockwork and we must finish a show feeling we've done everything within our power to provide the best value for money we can.

Of course I can't pot the balls for them but with at least two legends playing each night, and sometimes eight playing at a Legends Cup, they are not all going to forget where the pockets are.

We are also able to protect Ronnie. Sure, he has to make himself accessible to the people who pay for their VIP experience, but there is a line people can't cross. He doesn't find the hospitality side of it easy, but he understands he has to do it.

I've been a close friend of Ronnie for about five years now. Within Ronnie's snooker world, that almost warrants me a testimonial or a gold carriage clock for long service! In just that short time I've seen four or five managers come and go, close friends become strangers overnight, and witnessed the emotional struggles of maintaining a relationship with his family.

There is a side of Ronnie that most people never see; he is unbelievably generous, very funny and good company. He is also well-read and shows a real passion when he speaks on a subject that really interests him, cookery and running being the two obvious examples. Ask him about Mo Farah's split times over 5,000 metres, or his resting heart rate now compared to 2010 after a track session, and he won't be found wanting. He's also pretty good if you want to know where to enjoy the best food in East London – and he can usually get you a table sorted too!

Ronnie is also incredibly sensitive. I know he was upset at the way his own recent book got serialised. Even though he had no control on how they edited it, he was on the phone explaining to those who were cast in a light that was completely out of context how sorry he was.

The boring truth is in five years I've seen him drunk twice – well drunk I may add – and we've been out socially only a handful of times.

Outside of tournaments, and away from his 'work', he is a family man who dotes on his kids, does his running, likes to cook, and sits on the sofa drinking tea. I've seen Liam Gallagher text him to come for a drink, and David Beckham has asked for his number on more than one occasion. It simply doesn't interest him.

It doesn't make for rock and roll but that's the lifestyle that appeals to him. Maybe he did create hell before I met him but I have always thought the problem is the real Ronnie O'Sullivan is actually quite a boring fella who just happens to be the best in the world at what he does.

What he is guilty of, and I guess to a degree we all are, is morphing into the people who are around him at any one time. By that I mean he has various circles of friends, and he adapts his behaviour to suit the company he is in. I've seen the person Ronnie becomes in the company of his father for example; compare that to the guy who hangs around for seventeen days in Sheffield with artist Damien Hirst and you would swear it's only his physical appearance that is similar; surely this must be a hidden identical twin? The two personas are poles apart.

We hit it off from day one, mainly, I think, because I've never tried to change him or impose anything on him. I've never pressurized him into doing a show for me when commercially there were times I really needed him for ticket sales, and he knows it doesn't matter to me if he never plays a Legends show again.

Don't get me wrong. I have done a lot for him, both personally and commercially, but it's a two-way street.

Ronnie doesn't have a coach anymore, save Steve Peters. He is a player who performs on instinct. It's a natural ability with both hands that he has certainly worked at but can come very easily to him. The seemingly natural ability frustrates the hell out of his opponents as he can turn it on at a moment's notice.

Within his current trusted circle I am probably the most knowledgeable about the 'game' and we do talk about the technical aspects of snooker, especially when I am picking balls for him at tournaments.

He may be the best player in the world but he suffers the same self-doubt and anxiety as everyone else.

At work, he can be grumpy, impatient and rude, but as I say to him, he's been stuck in the same job for twenty-five years; you're bound to get pissed off with it once in a while aren't you?

And of course everything he does is magnified because of his commercial value to the sport. Everything Ronnie O'Sullivan does in snooker makes the papers. Without him the sport's commercial value to sponsors would suffer, as he proved when he took his last sabbatical.

But he is a free spirit, very much like Alex was in his day. He refuses to toe the line all the time and I'm sure if you ask Barry Hearn, honestly he would probably agree that it's not a bad thing for the sport.

There are few characters left nowadays – he is to snooker what Tiger Woods is to golf, what Phil Taylor is to darts, and what David Beckham was to football. However when Tiger dropped away there was Rory McIlroy, when Phil started losing there was Van Gerwen, and when Beckham retired, two blokes called Ronaldo and Messi filled the void. Seriously, within snooker who is going to fill the gap left by Ronnie O'Sullivan when he stops playing?

Sure, there are other good players, but you can't turn a Selby or a Murphy into a Ronnie. It's not in their nature and why should they change? Even Mark Selby would admit that though he may be World Champion, and wins many big tournaments, the sport is still primarily, at least from the media angle, all about Ronnie.

Will he turn up? How will he play? "Look, he lost", "look, he's cut his hair" – everything he does seems to be newsworthy.

Ronnie never chose to be famous; he just wanted to play snooker. It wasn't his fault that the job and career he chose came with all the other 'stuff' – stuff he is not that comfortable with even after doing it for over twenty years.

I first met him in 2010. We'd just finished our first Legends Tour and Jimmy was playing him in Colchester to raise money for Ronnie's PA who had breast cancer. Jimmy knew if he could get Ronnie involved, then not only would Legends have someone who could sell tickets like Alex Higgins, but the Whirlwind himself would be in for lots more work himself.

He was with a guy called Robbie who had shared a prison floor with Ronnie's father and had been tasked with helping Ronnie out. I got on with him straight away. He was very calmly spoken but what the fuck he knew about snooker I will never know!

That night Ronnie was quite quiet, subdued. The event certainly wasn't organized like a Legends night, and I think he would have quite happily have written a cheque for double the amount the night was going to raise to not have to play there at all. Jimmy gave up his night as well to play him; I think he played a few shows in prison for Ronnie as well. Ronnie would repay the favour by playing at Jimmy's testimonial. They'd give each other the shirt off their backs.

It's a very special friendship. First there was Alex, then Jimmy picked up the mantle. Ronnie carried on from Jimmy... After Ronnie it feels like we have a dodo situation looming. As Stephen Hendry said during the 2014 World, after Ronnie destroyed Shaun Murphy, "Will someone please step up?" – poignant words that refer to snooker as a whole now I think, rather than just that one particular tournament.

I was in the dressing room in Colchester but I felt like a bit of an intruder, the exact hanger-on I despise at my own events. I really had no purpose and kept quite quiet. Ronnie himself asked me if I did the Legend shows full-time; I explained that actually my company did mostly children's theatre, including the national tour of *Thomas the Tank Engine*.

"Little Ronnie loves that," he said. "Can you get me some tickets?"

"Fuck me," I thought, "I'll bring him to you and you can have a private viewing if you want!"

I exchanged numbers with Robbie and we set up some tickets for him to come to one of my shows at the Orchard Theatre in Dartford. Ronnie came with his mum, Maria, and his two children, Ronnie Junior and Lily.

It was a show I was pretty proud of. We'd used the trains from the worldwide tour and I'd reworked and rewritten the script for the UK stage. I'd also directed the performance.

To give you an idea, the Thomas train itself cost nearly $1 million to build, and it was only on loan. I didn't own it. I say this because we had to be very protective of it. Not only was it over a ton in weight and capable of eight miles per hour, but if it pushed you up against a wall it could kill you. The Health and Safety procedures around the operating of the train were extensive. Only our stage manager and the actor who drove the train in the show were allowed anywhere near it.

And then of course there was the latex face.

The latex face on Thomas costs about $100,000. It was fully animatronic and felt like real skin – not that you *ever* touched it mind you. It was so fragile that the moment Thomas was off stage, or in-between shows, a protective cover would go over it. If we damaged it in any way, or split the latex, you could not repair it. As well as the cover, signs always adorned the prop clearly stating, 'Under no circumstances must you touch the face'. If we had to do photo calls, or even maintenance, we had another member of the stage management team on hand to make sure that you never touched the face.

Don't touch the face, don't touch the face....

Photo call with Ronnie and his kids and what does his daughter do? Practically tries hanging herself off the face, pulling his mouth, pushing his eyes about.

It was one of those real awkward moments where panic spread around everyone on stage. Luckily no harm was done, but as a mickey take the next time I visited a performance of the show the sign had been changed. It still said: 'Please do not touch the face' and underneath in sharpie had been added: 'unless your dad plays snooker'.

It was very funny

After the performance, Ronnie said to me that we should do a few shows, Just two months later we did our first show in Blackburn and streamed it on the internet.

The date fitted perfectly as both Jimmy and Ronnie has been in Blackpool for the Sky Shootout the day before. They were both sharp, and boy did it show.

Of the eight frames they played they made six centuries. It was ridiculous. The good news is we had it on film – I've sold a fair few DVDs of that night I can tell you. Suddenly the snooker had been raised to a whole new level; these two played some of the best stuff I've ever seen.

Ronnie was now part of Snooker Legends. As we did more shows, our friendship grew and I started helping him out at a few tournaments.

We took snooker back to the Barbican in York, the year before World Snooker relocated the UK there, and the artist Damien Hirst came along.

It was a buzz having one of the world's richest artists there and the picture he did for me – I say picture, it was more of a squiggle but who cares! – is framed on my wall. He seems a really cool guy and is so good for calming Ronnie, especially in Sheffield.

Damien is also a snooker nut, and incredibly generous, but he really doesn't give a fuck, about anything. It's quite refreshing to see someone who has elevated themselves to such a position where they basically make up the rules. Some of the art he has done for Ronnie is priceless, and I know he did a very special piece for Stephen Hendry too.

I was around the team at the time he won the 2012 World's but I didn't go to the final. It was shortly after this that the story broke that Ronnie was going to take a break from snooker and was refusing to sign the player's contract.

Commercially this was very bad for snooker: the world champion and the game's most prized possession was putting his feet up because he had been advised that the player's contract was too restrictive. It was a mess and the truth is it could have easily have been sorted if Ronnie, Django (his manager at the time) and Barry Hearn had sat round a table and explained what each clause of the contract meant.

Then again if Ronnie had carried on playing we would never have had the 2013 comeback story that once again meant The Rocket made snooker history.

CHAPTER 11

Ted Lowe – The Godfather

"For those of you who are watching in black and white, the pink is next to the green."

There is a common recurring argument that generally pops up whenever a tournament is televised on any other channel than BBC: "Who's the best commentator?"

In some people's eyes you need to have played the game at the highest level to have the authority to commentate on it – hence why when Hendry, Davis or Parrott talk, it's tough to challenge it because they have been there and done it.

But playing at the highest level doesn't make Jimmy White a good commentator – in fact he is pretty average. And I'm sure once he retires you won't see the major broadcasters enter into a bidding war for Selby – obviously!

There is one widely regarded 'Daddy' of snooker commentary who set the standards by which everyone is now measured.

For anyone who grew up watching snooker on TV, Ted Lowe was a constant companion, his voice associated with so many great moments from the sport. His commentary started in the days of black and white TV; this is where the famous quote at the top of this chapter comes from.

Ted wasn't a player; he was the manager of the Leicester Square Hall, at the time the home of billiards and snooker. He was a close associate of the all-time great Joe Davis, the fifteen-time world champion.

One day, BBC's regular commentator Raymond Glendenning had lost his voice; Ted stepped in to cover Raymond, and he found himself remaining at the microphone for fifty years! Ted would commentate from the audience and so had to keep the level of his voice as low as possible so as not to disturb the players. Hence the 'whispering' style and subsequent nickname.

In the 1960s the controller of BBC2 was wildlife expert David Attenborough. He wanted something to show off this new colour TV service, and with its coloured balls and cheap production costs, snooker was ideal. Ted came up with the idea for the series *Pot Black*.

After Ray Reardon joined the tour, and Kirk Stevens played in the Crucible, I spoke to JV about getting Ted along to be a special guest when the tour went to Brighton as that was where he lived.

JV thought it was a marvellous idea, as without Ted, JV himself would have never got a break behind the microphone. Jimmy was also especially close to Ted and they enjoyed a bottle of Dom Perignon on more than one occasion after tournaments.

Ted loved the idea, but did explain he was ninety years old now so JV would have to help him if he got tired! He was also worried about how he was going to get home that late at night after the show. I believe his wife Jean was a bit younger but certainly way beyond driving age.

Jimmy stepped in and booked a limousine, with champagne of course, to bring Ted, Jean, her brother and his wife to the theatre. They even discussed leaving early so they could take the longer route along the coast.

"Best get two bottles," Jimmy remarked.

We were all lifted by Ted agreeing to come and join the team. Since Alex's death the Legends mood had been sombre.

Ted was renowned, and loved, for making the odd gaffe on air. As well as the black and white TV quote, he was once commentating on the great Fred Davis at the World Championship. Fred was sixty-four at the time and struggling to get one leg on the edge of the table in order to reach a long shot. He gave up and switched to play the shot with his other hand.

Ted uttered the immortal words live on the BBC: "Well Fred Davis is 64 now, he is getting on a bit and is having trouble getting his leg over." Not content with that he followed it up by saying, "He prefers to use his left hand instead."

Dennis tells the story at every exhibition and even after hearing it fifty times it still makes me laugh.

About a month before the show was due to play Ted called, the whispering voice like smooth treacle down the phone. He explained he'd been suffering from a bit of a cold and was worried he may not be able to make it unless he could shake it off. He wanted to record a message to play to the audience just in case. To be honest I wasn't overly worried but he said he'd record it anyway.

A few days later a letter arrived with an accompanying TDK C60 cassette tape! I guess Ted didn't have an iPhone!

The letter was beautifully handwritten from Ted himself but I had no machine that even played a cassette anymore so I placed it in the drawer.

He phoned the next day to make sure I had received it and apologized for the singing! Singing? Now the contents of the tape did intrigue me.

Ted was feeling a bit better but he was worried about all the autographs he would have to sign as he had arthritis in his hands. So we sent the pictures down in advance so he could sign them at his leisure.

At the Crucible for the early rounds the table is separated by a dividing 'curtain'. They call it the curtain but in reality it's a solid piece of scenery that is hoisted in and out before play and probably weighs half a ton. The photo I chose from the Muscroft Collection for him to sign was the famous shot when live on TV, as Ted was closing off the broadcast, the curtain started coming in. Ted was right underneath it. Instead of moving to avoid a collision, which could have put the camera out of focus, he simply bent his knees to avoid being hit on the head whilst still continuing to speak. What a professional! The moment was captured beautifully and Ted loved the idea of having that as his official photo.

Generally, modern-day players have a threshold on the amount of autographs they will sign before they walk off; it's probably boredom as much as anything. I don't think Jimmy has gone more than a day or so in the last thirty-five years when he hasn't signed at least one photo, train ticket, body part or piece of underwear!

Also by the time they get to the tenth or so request the signature itself starts resembling just a scribble. I've learnt the hard way in Legends not to try to get them to sign too many things in one go as the ones at the end become pretty unusable.

Then of course the moment you ask them to add anything more than just their name, like a dedication or 'best wishes' it becomes a real issue for some!

I understand before an important match, or during their meals or practice, then they shouldn't be expected to stop and do photos and autographs. But I think as long as it's managed correctly then a fan should never be turned down from getting their hero's signature.

Of course the invention of the 'selfie' has made it even worse. Ronnie, for example, doesn't mind doing the pictures, but what drives him mad are people not knowing how to use their phones. What was supposed to be a quick arm round him for a snap turns into a survival technique of sharing body warmth with a stranger whist someone struggles with the phone.

Ted Lowe signed every photo meticulously, and added the phrase 'memories of pleasure'. They became real collectors' items and it's one of the few pieces of snooker memorabilia I have that I really treasure.

The photos got returned to me, I called Ted to thank him and we talked about the pick-up time for the limousine. The show itself was only a few weeks away. I thought everything was fine.

Ted passed away on May 1st, and never got to commentate at the Snooker Legends show in Brighton.

Jimmy made sure his widow Jean got the limo ride, with champagne, and shed a tear like all of us when his voice from beyond the grave was played to the crowd in the Brighton Centre that night. It all felt like Ted had a premonition to record the message. JV was particularly emotional.

The 2011 tour continued on, and we went north of the border and visited Scotland for the first time. I'd booked a punishing schedule for my team, four venues in four days. London to Penrith, Penrith to Glasgow, Glasgow to Inverness, Inverness to Aberdeen!

JP saw an opportunity to fill the days playing some of Scotland's finest golf courses. He still says those few days with Dennis and Cliff, playing links golf in the day and snooker in the evenings, were his favourite times.

Dennis always partnered JP and Cliff would play with the local member who had got them on the course. It was usually only for a tenner but if Dennis and JP won, Cliff would hand it over graciously and the world would know the outcome, Dennis made sure of that.

If Cliff won – sometimes it happened! – then two scruffy fivers or a few coins would be pulled from Dennis's golf bag and passed over via a secret handshake in the car park. It was pretty competitive.

The tour ended in Grimsby on the 13th July. We played thirty-one dates in 2011 and the boys had made thirty-five centuries, including Jimmy's second 147 maximum break. It was a great year, but we'd lost Ted and John Parrott had also lost his manager, Phil Miller.

Phil was the man who discovered John at thirteen and stayed with him throughout his whole playing career. He was a real help to me in the early days. He attended a few shows and always tried to support what we were doing. Snooker lost another good man the day Phil Miller passed. JP lost a father figure.

CHAPTER 12

The Champions League Final 2011

Midway through the 2011 tour I booked a couple of Irish venues: Belfast in Northern Ireland for our Alex Higgins tribute night and Goffs in Kildare, home for many years to the Benson and Hedges Irish Masters.

Annoyingly there was a dead day between the two shows. That meant extra hotel costs for our touring party, which actually had six players on it, as Kirk had flown in again from Toronto and Ken had joined us. I got an approach from Dundalk FC about staging an event, and after checking out the map, I saw it lay perfectly between the two current Irish dates.

I usually work with theatres who have their own marketing departments and databases; this goes a long way to selling tickets. Although Dundalk was a football club I still assumed they would have a fan base of season ticket holders, and we were only looking to shift five hundred tickets to cover our costs.

They could fit the date in. Happy days... But then two things happened: Dundalk FC sold tickets about as well as they kept clean sheets, and Manchester United beat Schalke of Germany 6-1 in the semi-final of the Champions League and would face Barcelona FC on the night we were due to play this extra show. It was the Stoke FA Cup scenario all over again.

I managed to work with a local marketing lady who got us a complimentary hotel, which saved some money, and as I was on a fee to cover costs, I wasn't really worried.

JV and Ken were gutted. Both big Manchester United fans, they didn't want to work on the night their team played in a cup final, especially against the world's most glamourous opponents who had beat them previously in the 2009 final.

Of course Dundalk FC now had the perfect excuse as to why tickets weren't selling: the football match. When I tried explaining that to sell tickets, people first need to know the fucking event is on, it fell on deaf ears.

The solution was simple, but one which my event team weren't going to like. We'd play the exhibition in the afternoon and have a Champions League party at the hotel in the evening! It meant my event team finishing at midnight in Belfast and setting up at 7am in Dundalk; you can probably guess how popular I was! The €50 bribes were in force that night.

However, what seemed like a 'fill in' date, with no expectations and nothing but aggravation in its planning, actually turned into an historic show.

We get quite a few celebrities visiting our shows, usually because of their friendships with Jimmy. In Dundalk it was no different and we welcomed one guest who was certainly larger than life.

Glenn Ross, known by his nickname 'Big Daddy', was a former Irish strongman and powerlifter, having been Britain's Strongest Man on five occasions. He was also a snooker fan.

We soon found out that strong men don't shake hands, they hug! I seriously thought he'd put my back out and Jimmy felt winded – this bloke was enormous. When he asked Jimmy for his chalk as a memento at the end of the show The Whirlwind was happy to oblige; he didn't hang round for a second hug though – I'm not sure his spine would have taken it. A perfect gentleman and very quietly spoken, Glenn could have probably carried the snooker table out on his back.

In Dundalk it was Jimmy's turn to be the person the raffle winner would get to play – as usual he was thrilled!

We'd ended up with three hundred in. I was going to lose a bit of money as the football club now couldn't guarantee the fee they agreed in the contract, but it wasn't a catastrophe. There hadn't been anything spectacular about the snooker in the first half; it was quite cold in the room and the table was running slow. It felt weird doing a show in the afternoon and everyone seemed a bit uninterested and lethargic.

The raffle winner was pulled out and down came this middle-aged man, delighted to have got the chance to challenge the great Jimmy White. Jimmy duly presented the cue to him, at which point he told JV that he had his own cue and the Mrs had just gone to the car to get it. It was quite a funny moment and JV milked it.

Another little thing we do is put the winner's name up on the scoreboard so it looks all official. As usual JV enquired to his name. "It's Terry," he said. "What's your surname, bud?" said JV knowing that there are two lines of text on the software for the scoreboard so you can display the player's full name.

"I want to be known as Tornado Terry," he said, bold as brass. The room laughed. Was this guy having a laugh or was he being serious?

As we were still filling time for his 'wand' to arrive from the boot of some charabang in the car park, JV tried to see just how serious he was.

"So, Tornado, you know that's Tony Drago's nickname don't you?"

"I'm quicker than him," quipped Terry

"Shame she's not been a bit quicker getting your cue, Terry," said JV.

It was obvious the guy thought he could play a bit, and when the cue duly arrived the mandatory handshake took place and Terry won the toss.

"I'll let you break," said Tornado with a small touch of bravado in his voice. By now he must have put half a block of chalk on his tip. The professional player usually lets the amateur break off, bit of etiquette. Jimmy wasn't too pleased about being summoned to the table to break off.

Jimmy smashed the cue ball at about a hundred miles an hour into the back of the pack from the top cushion.

These frames aren't about the pros proving they can play. These are about someone playing their hero on a match table and winning a cue – unless of course you brought you own cue with you!

The balls split all over the table and Terry approached the table. There was purpose in his stride and he meant business. He didn't get past the baulk line when a rogue red ricochet off about twelve other balls and dropped in the middle pocket. The crowd fell about.

"Sit down, Tornado," said JV.

At that point Terry had no idea he'd be sitting down for a while, but at least he'd have the best seat in the house as a bit of snooker history was about to be made.

Jimmy potted seven reds and seven blacks and we had all started to get that maximum 147 break feeling.

Although all the reds were spread around the table it actually was a disadvantage to Jimmy, as he had to navigate after each red ball back to the black through a maze of other balls. Also one huge disadvantage of playing the break-off shot like he did is you cannot fail to send the pink ball up the table.

The pink in this frame was actually sat almost frozen to the baulk cushion. It made a clearance seem unlikely but we could all dream.

Remember, up to this point Terry hadn't even had a shot; we were on the verge of the first ever 147 being made from the break-off shot... but we had that pesky pink to overcome first.

Ten reds, then eleven... Before long we'd got to the yellow and the place was buzzing. Fortunately a member of the crowd had been recording the frame so history was at least being documented, albeit via a handycam shaking like an earthquake had struck. I would have said Tornado instead of Earthquake but Terry was sat quiet in his seat. You had the feeling that trip to the car to get his cue was going to be a wasted one!

By the time we got to the blue ball every shot was being met with a huge cheer. JV was trying to calm everyone.

Blue to pink was easy enough, but we would need an angle on the pink to travel the twelve feet up the table to the final black and a 147 break – nothing was a certainty, especially as Jimmy himself knew he was on the verge of making history.

In truth, he butchered the blue. It went in but he was straight on the pink and didn't have any angle at all. He paused. JV called for hush. The only shot he had was a reverse deep screw off the opposite cushion to get anywhere near the black. If you're not a snooker player, let me put it this way: it was bloody near an impossible shot!

Jimmy threw everything at it, the pot was made, part 1... JV sprung into life as the cue ball started on its reverse gear journey to the cushion.

"Go in, give us a chance... go on..."

The ball looked like it was slowing up but once it hit the cushion, the side Jimmy had placed on the ball pinged it across the table. The black was makeable. One shot and we would all have witnessed the first ever 147 from the break-off.

Those who have followed Jimmy's career closely will know that one black had already cost him a moment of history, in 1994 against Hendry. Ken, looking down from the balcony, had also suffered the agony of missing a final black at the 2000 Masters tournament for a maximum that would have yielded him an £80,000 sports car. Kirk and Cliff had known the feeling of making the 147; to be fair, so had Jimmy in 1992 against Drago.

We all held our breath. There was no money on offer, no sports car, not even a cheese sandwich, but none of that made this less important.

Jimmy nailed the black.

The place went wild and people were bouncing. Tornado Terry was more interested in knowing from JV if he got another frame!

We partied long into the night. Sure, Barcelona beat Man United 3-1 but no one seemed to really care! Plenty of the black stuff was consumed and Mr and Mrs Virgo did a duet with the band long into the early hours. We all had to remind ourselves that we had a show again the next day. It wasn't the first time that the sun had started coming up before I had gone to bed on a show night.

The story of Jimmy making the 147 from the break-off is now part of Legends history and although it gets mentioned a bit by Legends fans I'm pretty sure anyone who has shared a pint or a pie at Dundalk FC with Tornado Terry since then has heard the story far more.

We'll never know just how good a player 'Tornado Terry' was, and maybe that's how it should stay. He's part of snooker history too!

First Meeting *(Right)* Me pictured with my team and Jimmy the first night I met him and proposed a Legends Tour

First Lady *(below)* Our Referee Michaela Tabb, I knew right away we'd become great friends.

Clever Boy *(Below)* Alex Hurricane Higgins back playing in the Crucible Theatre for Snooker Legends. The day before he had discharged himself from hospital, and he still wears the identity bracelet on his right wrist with cuffs rolled up for all to see.

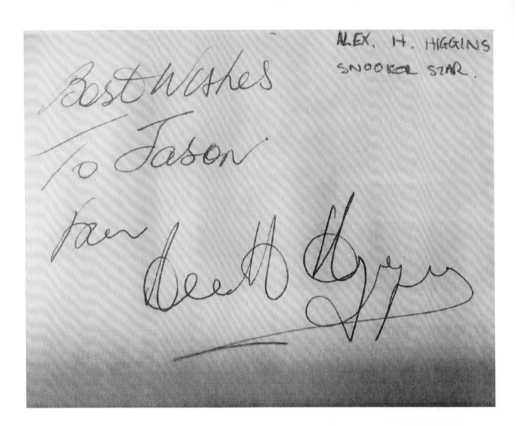

ALEX. H. HIGGINS
SNOOKER STAR.

Best Wishes
To Jason
from
[signature]

(*Above*) The autograph I got in 1981 from Alex. I wasn't there, in bed with ear ache.

(*Right*) My stepson Rowan with the World Trophy. It lived in my house for months.

(*Below*) The 1988 Cornwall U21 Snooker Champion!

The Glue *(Left)* John Virgo doing his impressions.

Bullseye *(Above)* Great show, didn't sell tickets

First Show *(Below)* The line-up; Alex made us wait until he was ready

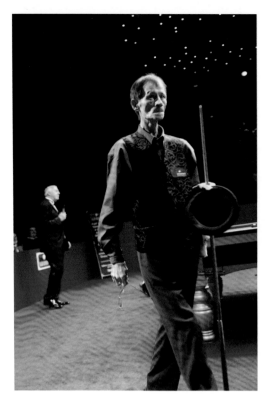

Appreciation *(Left)* Alex got his moment with the crowd in the Crucible. Dressed in a green shirt and waistcoat and with his hat, a la 1982

The Champ *(Right)* Ten times Ladies World Champion Reanne Evans who I now manage

The Team *(Right and Below)* Everyone at Legends is part of a team. Michelle, Georgie and Paul (known as T Bag) have been there from the start

Bazza *(Left)* With Barry and Sue Hearn at Jimmy's testimonial

The Boys *(Below)* Leighton and Matthew, our table fitters

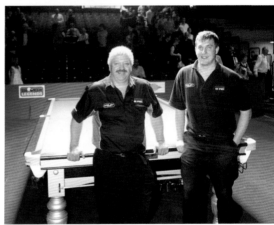

The new image for Reanne (Left)

World Champion *(Left)* Jimmy wins the 2010 World Seniors Championship. It was great to be there that night

The Man in the White Suit
(Above, Right & Below) It was
great to see Kirk Stevens back at
the Crucible

Dracula *(Above, Right and Below)* Ray was our special guest in Plymouth. He turned up three hours early to practice

Laughter *(Above)* Having fun in Plymouth

Burlesque *(Left)* A standard night out with Michaela and her husband!

Friends (Below Left) Cliff and Dennis, buddies since 1973

Comedy *(Below)* John Virgo doing a Dennis impression

Surprise *(Above, Right and Below)* At the end of the first tour the Legends surprised me and put me in the doubles; they even smuggled my cue up. They presented me with a memento of our eighteen shows as well. Special moments.

(Top) Ronnie and Tony the night after Liverpool. He should have been in Heathrow to fly to China

(Top Right) Travelling with The Rocket

(Right) Referee Jan, always top bloke to work with.

(Below) The Roket Fuel Energy Drink

(Bottom Right) Michaela's new look!

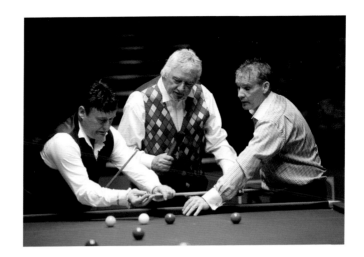

The Hero *(Right)* PC David Rathand who was blinded by Raoul Moat played at Legends in 2011

New Additions *(Left)* With Steve, Stephen and Ronnie on board we had a formidable line-up

Ronnie's first show for Legends *(Right)*. Six centuries in eight frames, it was amazing

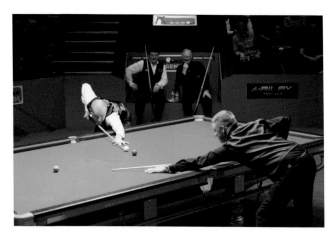

Mischief *(Right)* Steve and Stephen potting the colours against the clock with alternate shots

Hillsborough *(Below)* Ronnie and Jimmy showing their support for the families of the Hillsborough Victims.

Vlaar *(Right)* Aston Villa Captain Ron Vlaar came to a show and played; big snooker fan, not a bad player

Legends *(Left)* The world's two most popular snooker players.

History *(Left)* Cliff and Steve didn't really speak for eighteen years. Here they share a laugh and a drink at Legends with Ray

Popular *(Right)* Michaela is always popular in our VIP Reception!

Steve Davis *(Below)* having fun with the crowd at Legends in Sheffield

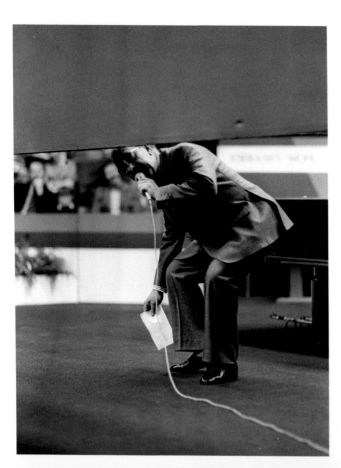

Whispering Ted Lowe
(Left) The famous picture capturing the moment the 'curtain' divider in the Crucible dropped while he was live on air.

Team *(Below)* Even Jimmy has to lend a hand with the event set-up sometimes.

(Top Left) The Snooker Legends Limousine

(Top Right) Footballer John Terry was our guest in Guildford

(Left) Doing Men's Cancer Awareness Day with Jimmy and Peter Andre

(Below) Tony arriving for filming of his documentary

Strongman *(Left)* Glenn Ross joined us in Dundalk; lovely gentle fella but almost broke my spine.

Dennis *(Below)* trying a new trick shot!

Stones *(Below)* A surreal lunch with Jimmy, Ronnie Wood and Charlie Watts. Once again, instead of getting in the picture I was taking it.

Tattoo *(Below)* Derby Legends: a loss would have meant Mark Williams having to get a tattoo on his backside

(Above) The King of the Crucible

(Right) Oval Vodka Photo Shoot

(Below Right) The trophy we gave to PC Rathband

(Below) Me and Stevie G!

(Top) Ronnie and fellow Stone Bill Wyman

(Top Right & Above) Ronnie and Mick put on a superb concert

(Right) The Testimonial team and I did an eighteen-hour day

(Below Right) We made the place look as best we could with no budget

(Above Left) Relaxing before a show

(Above) Mark saved from getting the tattoo

(Left) These two bicker like an old married couple

(Below) Jimmy, Ronnie and artist Damien Hirst

(*Above*) Snooker Legends turned out for Jimmy's day.

(*Below*) Old friend Tony Meo with Ken at the Testimonial

(Top) Michalea advertising our Goffs Baseball Caps!

(Above) I called my snooker club in Newbury The Crucible

(Top Right) Having Dinner with Cliff, Dennis, Tony & Alain

(Right) At World Seniors, Dene O'Kane from New Zealand

(Bottom Right) Before Snooker Legends I was in a comedy double act, and yes I am wearing a fat suit!

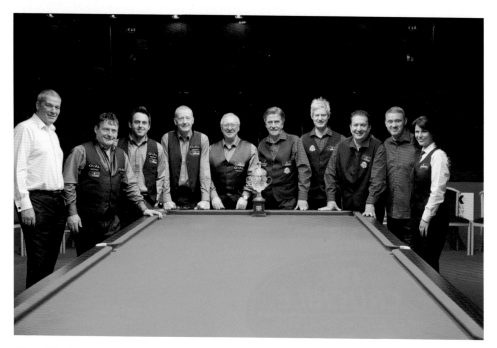

(Above) The Line up for Legends Cup on Eurosport

(Below) Busy night in Liverpool, 1500 were in.

(Above) Jonathan Kendrick, Chairman of the Rok Group that financed Ronnie's return to the sport in 2013

(Below) The press conference I organized, sat with Ronnie and Jimmy facing the world's Media.

(Above) Stephen wasn't used to being in a Team. It showed!

(Above right) The Tornado was pumped up and followed every match.

(Right) Me and fellow director Nick George with our hands on the World Trophy.

(Below) Cliff pots a black during the fight back and Tony jumps on him!

(Above) Friends since 1973 – but desperate to beat each other

(Above) Bedworth was a great venue for the first staging of the Legends Cup

(Right) Down on the black ball re-spots and the banter was flying

(Below) Dennis celebrated potting the final black

(Below) I had the job of doing the thank you speech to all concerned.

(Left) Me with the Great WT at Jimmy's bash

(Above) Ronnie's Ferrari, he lent it to me!

(Below) After winning the world's he offered the trophy up, it felt nice to have played a part in the comeback story

(*Above*) Joe Johnson joined Legends, complete with pink shoes from 1986!

(*Top Right*) The Grinder looking immaculate as usual at the 2013 Seniors

(*Right*) The 9 Ball pool table we got installed at Melwood, Liverpool FC's training ground.

(Above Left) Pure Box Office.

(Above) JP and Tony, as usual Tony would be chatting.

(Left) The Tabbster

(Below) The First Choice Line up

(Top Left) It was pretty cool setting Sky to record my own show

(Left) The Legends girls started becoming famous in their own right

(Above) Cliff took great delight in beating Ronnie in a frame at Legends Cup

(Below Left) Drago was emotional

(Below) Robertson was a great addition.

(Above) It was a set-up rather bigger than we were used to

(Below) The scene was set, live to 12.3 million.

(Above) I interview Ronnie and Michaela Live for Eurosport.

(Right) Neil almost gives Tony a concussion as they celebrate the win.

(Below) The England and Northern Ireland Team.

(Top) Cliff and his winning team thank me live on air, special moment.

(Above) Tony was dancing, JV worked so hard that weekend.

(Right) Ronnie and I after he won the Champion of Champions in Coventry in 2014. We laughed all week

(*Above*) Filming with Drago in Valetta, Malta.

(*Below Left*) Meeting Tony's friends and enjoying Rabbit.

(*Below Right*) Relaxing with Ronnie, he is drinking tea as usual!

(*Top Left*) Legends at the Crucible.

(*Above*) Drago was great to film he wasn't too keen on flying!

(*Left*) 6 Red Pool, will it ever happen?

(*Below*) Seven year old Westley Cooper stood on a box to play Hendry in the Crucible!

There is no sound in snooker as great as a full house in Goffs!

(Above) The Captain, Ali Carter, battling Ireland not cancer for once

(Right) Joe Swail – great with the fans

(Left) Fergal and Ken

(Above) Two great Legends, two great friends.

(Left) Legends Night with a difference to celebrate Stephen's 25 years since winning the title.

(Below) Ronnie reacts to beating Joe Perry at 2014 Worlds, he wore my patch for the whole tournament.

(Above) Reanne Evans, I'm convinced she can be a top 64 player.

(Top Right) Trying to resurrect the UK Pro-Am Circuit.

(Right) My mate Andy got to partner Hendry at the Crucible. Andy and I own a snooker club by the same name.

(Below) The new snooker app I helped bring to market. It could change the way people play cue sports forever.

PLAY LIKE A CHAMPION
WITH THE WORLD'S FIRST CUE WITH
BUILT-IN SIGHTING & ALIGNMENT
TECHNOLOGY FOR ALL CUE SPORTS

(Above) Ronnie feeling a little worse for wear at the first Legends Cup!

(Right) Sewing on the logo as Audley Harrison looked on.

(Bottom Right) The £5000 Vodka Bottle.

(Below) Dennis laughing, for a change!

(Above) Clear to see who looks best for his age!

(Left) The App banner that caused so much fuss

(Below Left) The iPhone covers!

(Below Centre) Tony played an exhibition at my club, not a bad six frames!

(Below right) I watch on as Ronnie enters the VIP

CHAPTER 12A

Steffhan, The King of the Crucible

Many of the Legends I've worked with have superstitions, and as you can see by the numbering of this particular chapter, I'm afflicted by one as well. Some players are terrified of changing their pre-match routines: they always put a certain match shoe on first, or they save a lucky shirt for finals etc. For me I grew up fascinated by space, or more importantly the Apollo space program that took Neil Armstrong to the Moon in 1969. Apollo 13 was slated to be the third moon landing but a defective oxygen tank meant it became more about a race to get home and save the lives of Astronauts Lovell, Haise and Swigert. After that tragedy no other spacecraft, or NASA mission has ever carried the number thirteen. From the age of seven, when I first read about this, I decided to follow suit.

Stephen Hendry has become part of the Snooker Legends family, so much so the girls get away with calling him Steffhan – and he answers to it!

He may well be the most decorated player in snooker history but in a career where it's all about excelling as an individual, Stephen seems to really enjoy being part of a team, where he accepts that he is no more important than anyone else in the team that puts the show on, be that the technician T Bag (Paul), the table fitter Leighton, or Michelle, Georgie, Lauren or Tash, the 'legendary' girls who run the hospitality at our events.

Snooker Legends works because of the team ethic. It's not unusual when we are away on tour to find any of our players helping out during the day with the set-up of our show. Jimmy even grabs the hoover sometimes.

I think they almost enjoy spending the day in the venue creating the event, rather than replicating the years of touring where if they weren't playing matches they would stare at hotel walls waiting for them.

We all work hard and play hard. We produce the very best show we can and then it's great as a team to relax and unwind after the show over a pizza (Tabby's fault) and a beer, or in Stephen's case the finest red wine the Premier Inn stocks!

Never before have you seen a man more content with his retirement from professional snooker, and it's a contentment I know Ronnie is jealous of. Here is a man who sacrificed most of his childhood and adult life to being the very best at what he did. Now it's a period of down time, a time almost to enjoy letting people see a more 'human' side of him rather than the ruthless winning machine he was in the 1990s.

Stephen and Jimmy are especially close on tour, which is weird when you consider just how much a nemesis to Jimmy he was. Then again Stephen played a huge part in creating the 'people's champion' tag Jimmy now carries. 'Seven times' won the titles and picked up the cheques; Jimmy won the fans and picked up the birds!

I've been privileged to spend time in the company of both of them and much as Jimmy wanted to win the World's, he is almost loved more, and therefore you could say he has earned more from the demand for exhibitions by not winning one.

It was Jimmy who got Stephen involved in year three of the tour. He set up a meeting for me at Alexandra Palace at the Masters. At the time Stephen was in the last year of his career, but no one knew it at that point. He shuffled into the players' room in a screwed up check shirt, unshaven and a flat cap. I assumed it was his day off... but he was in fact on his way to commentate!

We booked three shows, the first a clash at the Crucible with Jimmy, followed by a match at Preston Guildhall, another great snooker venue, two days later.

At that point, we knew the fate of both of their 2012 World Championship qualifiers would be known, or at least we thought so. Not for the first time, but I accept not on purpose, World Snooker changed the qualifying dates for the championship so Jimmy and Stephen would have their final qualifying matches on our Preston date. I had to consider the fact that both would be battling for a place at the World Championships on the night I had sold eight hundred tickets for in Preston.

Thankfully Freya at World Snooker reduced the risk for me by having both players play their final session of the match in the afternoon, but it still meant if the match was close that they would struggle to get to Preston on time.

Sadly Jimmy lost on the Thursday, and really having to stay for the Legends on the Friday night was torture, as it was the last place he wanted to be – but of course this Jimmy was very different from the one I had first met in 2009 and there was no way he would let me down.

Stephen was drawn to play Yu DeLu, a young Chinese player, and went 7-2 up in the first session race to 10 on the Saturday afternoon. This was good news as it meant that he only needed three frames for another World Championship appearance.

He rattled them off on the Sunday afternoon, jumped in his car and arrived in Preston fifteen minutes before our VIP reception. Naturally he was buzzing, but he knew how much losing had meant to Jimmy so he really contained himself. That showed real class; massive respect. Jimmy was the first to congratulate him as well.

The Preston night went great and after the pack up we returned to the hotel to find Stephen waiting up with drinks for everyone. He immediately fitted in and obviously felt comfortable enough to confide in me that he was going to 'retire' at the Crucible. At that point I think only his close family, Jimmy and I knew, so I suddenly felt slightly humble to have been trusted with this secret.

I don't know if he was telling me to let me know he was free for work or whether he just felt comfortable sharing the news knowing there was still work playing snooker after leaving the professional tour in a more relaxed atmosphere with us.

He also told us he had agreed a deal with JOY in China to launch their Chinese Black 8 pool game which would see him over there playing Black 8 exhibitions almost on a monthly basis.

When the news broke, after he lost to Stephen Maguire, World Snooker weren't happy. I even heard comments that they thought he had turned his back on the game that made him who he was.

The reality was there were only four players left with any commercial market value: Ronnie of course, Davis, Jimmy and Stephen. With Jimmy and Davis in a rankings freefall, and Ronnie firmly in 'may play'/ 'may not play' mode, they were losing an asset. Sad they couldn't wish him well like his peers did with a guard of honour in the Crucible during the championship.

Of course he didn't retire quietly, just producing the tenth 147 of his career against Stuart Bingham, then beating fellow Scot John Higgins before defeat to Maguire. It takes quite a lot to walk away when you've once again proved over the longer match format, under the intense pressure of a Crucible crowd, that you are still one of the top eight players in the world. I know even if he had won it he was off. A new life beckoned.

Barry Hearn was never a Stephen Hendry fan, the real reason being that he was never able to manage or control him. While Stephen dominated the game Barry had no choice, with regards to Matchroom matters, but to pander and work with Ian Doyle and his 110 Sport Management, who mentored and managed Stephen.

Barry discovered Steve Davis who won six world titles. Ian Doyle discovered Stephen who won seven world titles. Barry was second best... ouch!

You could say Barry had the last laugh as Ian Doyle and 110 Sport Management went bankrupt, but during the 1980s and 1990s, I think Stephen and John Parrott were the only two top players to not at some time have been under the control of Matchroom.

I have no idea what Stephen gets paid in China – it's none of my business – but I do know it will be a damn sight more than I can ever pay him for a Legends show. He is treated like royalty out there, like a king: stays at the best hotels, eats at the top restaurants.... In truth, luckily for me, he seems just as content with a takeaway pizza, a glass of red and the Premier Inn! He must enjoy our shows!

During his time as a professional player I don't think Stephen had a 'best mate' on tour; he was too interested in winning to care. The closest person to him was, I believe, Mark Williams, himself a two-time world champion. Mark appeared in the very first year of Legends but hadn't appeared since, and was keen to do a show with Stephen. I set up a match at The Assembly Rooms in Derby for Stephen and Mark to take on Steve Davis and Jimmy. Mark is a wind-up merchant: he is a master on social media of being the cause of trouble or argument and then stepping away to avoid the flack. It works most of the time. It didn't work when he criticised the Crucible Theatre and got an £8,000 fine!

In the build-up to this event Mark had stated on Twitter that if Stephen and himself lost to Jimmy and Steve, he would have a tattoo done on his backside saying 'I love Nugget'.

What was a flippant remark almost came back to haunt him big time as I made the very most of his tweet to get the maximum publicity out of it. They did win but not before a lot of drama where Stephen refused to take this impending date with the tattoo needle seriously. Twice on re-spotted blacks Stephen was trying to cut the ball in from the break. The normal confident Welsh Potting Machine was twitching for sure, not helped by Steve making buzzing sounds when he was down on the shot. The great thing about Mark is that I have no doubt he would have done it had they lost. Mark is probably his best mate in snooker but that doesn't mean Stephen won't take any opportunity to wind him up.

Moving forward, Stephen has a pivotal role in how Legends will develop. With him on board I am not so reliant on Ronnie to sell tickets. He showed me incredible loyalty in Germany when he saw I was being screwed over. I can't think there will have been many occasions in a career spanning twenty-five years that he has travelled overseas on a three-day playing trip and refused to take any payment for it? Of course he also met his current partner on our tour so I guess that helps a bit.

He has stepped beautifully into the commentary team at the BBC, probably at Willie Thorne's expense, and he has earned the respect of seasoned pros like Dennis and Virgo because he talks such sense and isn't afraid to upset the current professionals.

I hope that participation in the Legends events form part of his plans for the next few years, alongside his commentary and of course his commitments in China. The only problem I can see is that the demand is there to make some of our events more competitive, something I know he won't be interested in, and why should he? He has nothing to prove to anyone.

I'd like to think people at Legends have already seen a different side of him. He certainly likes to 'dish' out the verbals to Steve Davis and is fantastic meeting the public – nothing like the dour moody winning machine of the 1990s!

I was honoured that he accepted the captain's role for the 2014 Legends Cup Team; he was up against Jimmy White's team. Jimmy's team slaughtered them. Guess the Whirlwind finally got some payback.

Look up 'retirement and contentment' in the sporting dictionary and my hunch is you'll find Stephen Hendry's name.

CHAPTER 14

The Testimonial – Jimmy White

In 2012 Jimmy White would turn fifty years old; he would also celebrate thirty years as professional snooker player. Two good reasons to stage a testimonial – with the third, of course, being he could make himself some extra dough!

By the end of the 2011 tour we'd become close friends and although he had signed a management deal with Paul Mount at On Q Promotions, the reality was that Paul was never going to be able to manage Jimmy. He was more a figurehead for his new Snooker Academy in Gloucester.

Jimmy White is unmanageable; more than thirty years of feeling ripped off and abused by those who may claim the same thing about him have left him quite untrusting of people – especially people within the game of snooker.

When he first asked me to organize a testimonial I was a bit taken back, as really it was something that his manager should have been doing. It was a huge challenge but one that I would relish. It was also one hell of a responsibility to take on.

I knew Jimmy was loved, and I knew I could put on a good event. It certainly didn't turn out as we both expected, but it was a great lesson for Jimmy in learning who his friends really were.

I wanted at least a year to sort this. We ended up with nine months and one testimonial in essence became two as we did a lunch and evening event – madness really when I reflect upon it.

Our problem, which was actually a good problem to have, was that Ronnie O'Sullivan had agreed to play a snooker exhibition for him, and Ronnie Wood of the Rolling Stones had agreed to sing for him. Both offers were too good to turn down but there was no synergy between the two, even though of course Ronnie Wood is a huge snooker fan, and the two Ronnies and Jimmy have formed a formidable trio when out on the drink together.

The only answer was to stage two events: have a lunch with a snooker exhibition, then get rid of the snooker table and have a dinner and pop concert. Jimmy wanted to do it at the Grosvenor House in London, in the Great Room. That immediately put the event under huge financial stress as hire costs alone were tens of thousands.

My idea was to invite every living World Snooker Champion along to host a table for Jimmy. It would help promote the event and give the fans a chance to meet a whole host of snooker stars.

Jimmy had shared the jungle with chef Gino D'Acampo and he agreed to design the menu for the two events; the cost alone was £50-£60 a head to us. I felt it was too much. Jimmy's fan base was more pie and mash, and here we were debating a drizzle of this and a smear of that. It felt a bit snobbish.

With every snooker champion bringing a guest and getting a complimentary room at the Grosvenor as a thank you, we were already looking at a bill in excess of £50,000. I was worried so I called a meeting at Jimmy's house with his accountant, who was a fellow director of the testimonial committee, and his daughter Lauren. I felt I needed help and contacts, and there was only one man for the job, Barry Hearn.

Jimmy phoned Barry and he agreed to come on board. I met with Barry two or three times and he helped set the table prices. He also bought two tables for Matchroom and gave us a great prize for the auction: tickets for a host of sporting events. He also allowed us to announce the event at the final of the 2011 Masters, but the BBC stopped that being broadcast, and the commentators were stopped from saying why Jimmy was in the audience that night. Petty really when you think how many viewers had turned onto the BBC over the years because Jimmy was playing.

You could buy a Premier Table hosted by a former World Snooker Champion for eight people for £8,000 all day, or £3,000 for lunch and £6,000 for dinner. You also got a signed cue from Jimmy. It seemed very expensive to me, with tickets averaging about £375 each. An 'Event table' could sit ten: you didn't get the celebrity but you did get a cue. That was £5,000 for all day.

Looking back I think we should have just done the evening event with the

Ronnie Wood concert. As much as people love seeing Ronnie O'Sullivan play snooker, you can pretty much see that at a Legends show.

From the very start people were only really interested in buying tables for the evening. Jimmy was staggered when a few of the world champions we'd invited presented us with bills for their flights. Sure it was only a couple hundred quid but it hurt him. Here was a man who had helped create the prize money in the 1980s they had all got rich on in the 1990s. He also remarked that he'd got at least a dozen exhibitions for each of these guys over the years and not asked for a penny.

After we launched at the Masters final I got about £30,000 pledged in tables. It was nothing really, and Jimmy and I endured six months of stress that we only shared between ourselves, trying to get people to commit.

Outwardly we proclaimed that bookings were going well, it was going to be a great night and people needed to get their table secured. We had a minimum number set by the hotel, so if we didn't sell that number we'd be paying for those dinners anyway. While this was going on, Jimmy was also fighting for his place on tour as a professional snooker player, and his gout was flaring up again, making it painful to walk.

People who Jimmy had worked with for years suddenly couldn't make that night. Excuses like "I'd like to, Jimmy, but business has been slow" became a recurring theme. The simple fact was, Jimmy White fans were not the sort of people who spend £375 on a meal at the Grosvenor Hotel.

The Grosvenor was the wrong place to stage it. That was partly my fault but you couldn't really ask Ronnie Wood to play in a sports hall, could you? The event to celebrate one of the world's greatest ever snooker players had to have some kudos, and Jimmy wanted a Central London location.

Because of the pressure of not selling tables, we had no money to spend on the event itself. I cut together a twenty-minute DVD from footage showing the highlights of Jimmy's career; it was acceptable but certainly not professional. I really could have done with being able to use some of Barry's production team at Matchroom. We tried to get memorabilia on show, like Jimmy's jungle uniform, and he agreed to auction basically everything he had, including his cue. I got my designer to print off some nice photographs from his career.

We really were trying to make it look good, but everything now had to be about making as much money from the people who were attending the event, as it was obvious we weren't going to sell all the tickets.

In January I first made contact with the Rolling Stones office. Obviously having Ronnie Wood play was going to need some organizing. Up to this point, though, Jimmy and I thought that it would be Ronnie sat on a stool with an acoustic guitar.

What we ended up with was far bigger and better, but it no longer came for free! Shirley at the Stones office told me that Ronnie was putting together a band for the night and they had all agreed to play for free. Amazing, I thought, especially when we got told that Ronnie would be joined on stage by fellow Stones Bill Wyman and Mick Taylor, and the front man would be no other than Mick Hucknall from Simply Red.

Ronnie Wood's son, Jesse, was going to work with me on logistics and it soon became clear that although the band would perform for free, the bill for all the rehearsals, their personal expenses, studio hire, and all the sound and light costs were going to have to be picked up by Jimmy himself from the testimonial income!

Jimmy felt too embarrassed to tell Ronnie Wood. I was also told by Shirley that all the band members, except Ronnie, had to be given £1,000 in cash in an envelope on the night to cover their expenses.

One minute I was being told how lucky we were to have Mick Hucknall playing, as he usually charged £150,000 per appearance, and the next thing I'm being told to stuff an envelope with £1,000 as Mick's about to get his taxi and wants his expenses! The bloke could sing, but aside from that he was pretty unpleasant to all my team. I could certainly find better ways to spend one hundred and fifty thousand quid, that's for sure.

To cut a long story short, Ronnie Wood's involvement in the testimonial cost us about £20,000, save some change. While the joint rocked, and people danced to some of rock and roll's biggest legends, only Jimmy and I knew the full picture. We paid for everything from the twenty-four cans of Red Bull in the green room for the band, right down to a driver and amp for Bill Wyman. Thank God most of them were reformed alcoholics and no longer drinking, or it could have been even worse.

The other issue was that although all of Jimmy's so-called friends were not able to buy tables and tickets to support him, they were able to come out of the woodwork to ask for free ones.

On top of the tickets for the snooker players, who were hosting tables, we did a free table for his manager Paul and his sponsor – no problem at all with any of that.

However the whole lunch became farcical as people turned up on the door asking for Jimmy and trying to get in for free. I was fucking furious: this was the Grosvenor Hotel not some bloody exhibition in Tooting.

Also, logistically, we had a meticulous table plan. Jimmy was being made to let people in, and chairs were being pulled up to tables with guests asking for place settings. Much as I would love to name names in here it wouldn't be fair to Jimmy. He knows exactly who turned up, and the extra £3,000 he spent buying dinners for freeloaders and 'old friends' didn't get forgotten. Many 'old friends' probably think it's weird why they no longer hear from Jimmy, or why he no longer takes their calls. It was disgusting.

Also originally planned for the night was impressionist and singer Joe Longthorne, another friend of Jimmy. The plan was after dinner Joe would go on and get the crowd going, and then we'd do the auction before Ronnie Wood played.

Also, for reasons I will never understand, Jimmy had asked a dodgy Elvis tribute act to close the night. I pleaded with him to just get a DJ in, and Barry Hearn knew DJ Spoony, but Jimmy had asked 'The King of Rock and Roll' in a drunken moment at a previous show and felt he couldn't disappoint the lad.

To be fair following Ronnie Wood and Mick Hucknall was never going to be easy, but these guys were nothing more than average, and this was far and away the biggest gig they had ever played – it was a bit embarrassing and the dance floor was empty. Burning Love it was certainly not, more Suspicious Minds!

We had some fantastic auction items: a cue painted by famous artist Damien Hirst and a round of golf in Florida donated by Ian Poulter. Messrs. Wood, Hucknall and Wyman also signed guitars, one of which was given to Talksport's Andy Goldstein for hosting the event.

But I had a problem. Joe Longthorne was ill the night before the show. So without Joe, I either went straight to the auction after dinner, which felt a bit mercenary, or we let them have Ronnie Wood, get them up dancing and feeling like they had a great night, and then hit them with a chance to spend.

I put Ronnie Wood on. It was a big call, and Barry said, "Great night, Jason, but you've fucked your auction." The truth is, I think there was only a certain amount of money in the room and we would have got it either way. Barry was probably right though.

Willie Thorne did the auction for Jimmy. Undoubtedly there was no one better to do it and raise the maximum amount of money, but Willy cannily negotiated himself a fee for doing so.

It was an amazing night for Jimmy and his family, and it did celebrate him turning fifty and thirty years in the game. Sadly it didn't really make Jimmy any money, but he found out who his friends really were.

I speak to Jimmy every day, sometimes two or three times a day, certainly more than I speak with my girlfriend! He's one of my best friends in the sport and I've been his unofficial manager for the last five years. By unofficial I mean I don't get paid for it!

Reading his recent book, cleverly titled *Second Wind*, I don't know the man who talks about what he did in the 1980s and 1990s. I can certainly believe it, but it's not the bloke I know to be one of my best friends today.

He says he's wasted about four million on gambling, drink, drugs and having a good time. For a man who lived in world of cash exhibitions I reckon it's nearer double that.

Jimmy thinks he is a changed man because he has not taken cocaine for fifteen years and that he hardly ever has a drink. With mobile phones, cameras and social media he certainly could never get away with what he did in those days in the modern era. We often laugh about what Alex Higgins would have been like on Twitter or Facebook – absolute mayhem.

One of Jimmy's biggest qualities is his generosity. If I was ever in trouble he would be my first call, and I know he would do whatever he could to help me.

Sadly I know the day when Jimmy White no longer plays professional snooker is not too far away; it's something he refuses to contemplate. I have no idea how he will cope with that but I'll be there for him, trying to keep him involved in the sport that's been his life, through my Legends shows.

Jimmy can be found in life's dictionary under the description for 'No Regrets'. Asked if he would do it all again the same way, he simply says, "What do you think?"

The Whirlwind may not blow quite as hard as it once did but he will forever be regarded as part of snooker's royalty.

Those South London roots will never completely go away; Jimmy is always looking for a deal, an angle, a swerve. He must be the director or shareholder in a hundred companies, many of which promised him millions and ended up bankrupt. He's been a drug taker, a drinker, a gambler, bankrupt and a bad husband... He's also a great father, a generous friend, raised thousands for charity and done more free shows for good causes than I care to remember. He never turns down an autograph or a photo, although it is fair to say he'd prefer to sell you one of his. I've seen him up after winning matches and down after getting beaten – sadly he gets beat more than he wins these days and the hurting gets worse.

But mention the name Jimmy White to people on the street and they immediately smile. He has that effect on people. He has that effect on me.

CHAPTER 15

The Return of The Rocket

During Ronnie's 'retirement from professional snooker' we planned an October tour of six Legends shows and didn't just talk about creating our own 'Ronnie challenges...' series. The issue of forming a breakaway association from World Snooker began taking shape.

Even though Ronnie was adamant he was not going to play again, I was still not going to start booking theatres for shows that clashed with the major tournaments in the calendar. If history had taught me anything I knew that Ronnie could be guilty of the odd change of mind!

He had signed a contract with Merlin Entertainments and left Grove Leisure. Merlin is the management company of cricketer Freddie Flintoff and former footballer Jamie Redknapp. Ronnie had met them whilst appearing as a guest on the Sky show *A League of Their Own*. The idea was Merlin were going to help develop his media career away from snooker, and we were going to carry on working directly, like we always had, on the Legends shows.

People say Ronnie is difficult to manage, and they point to the number of managers he has gone through during his career as proof of this. People like Django at Grove have successfully managed Judd Trump and Neil Robertson, and in the early days Ronnie was managed by Barry Hearn himself. Those two could argue that they are proven managers of successful players.

Generally players pay a percentage of their table earnings to their managers; to my knowledge Ronnie never has. His argument, and it's a valid one, is that they cannot affect what he does on the table, so why should they share in that income?

Sure, if they are providing an administration service, or coming to events to assist, booking hotels, then I agree it should not be costing them, and to be fair I don't think it ever has. Ronnie is stupidly generous.

The opportunity for Ronnie's manager to earn comes from the off-table commercial deals, or the logo patches they can deliver because of who Ronnie is and what he has won on the table.

However, having Ronnie O'Sullivan in your stable means you will attract other players to your management who *will* pay you a percentage of tournament winnings. As their off-table commercial value is so much lower they cannot provide their managers with income that way.

What I do disagree with, and what I believe has happened with previous managers in the past, is to use a commercial approach for Ronnie and divert it to another player you manage because you'll earn a higher percentage from the deal you have with them.

Ronnie has the occasional 'mad' moment. For example, he signed an exclusive management deal with Merlin without even reading the contract, or getting someone else to read it. Just like his game he lives on instinct, using a sixth sense of right and wrong. But contracts are twenty-five pages for a reason, and not for the first time when Ronnie decided he no longer wanted to be with Merlin, he found the contract clauses were going to make that divorce pretty expensive.

In about September 2012 we did a show in Ipswich, and Ronnie told me the contract issues were sorted and he was going to play a bit again. He entered a small PTC Event in Gloucester and the International Tournament in China.

The last date of our tour was going to be played in Liverpool, a town very dear to Ronnie, where he lived for a couple of years when he first was turning pro.

The tournament snooker attendances and particularly the Premier League Snooker on Sky were suffering because Ronnie wasn't in it. While we packed in 1,500 people at the Echo Arena in Liverpool, the Premier League match in Guildford, live on Sky with Bingham and Ebdon, had about a hundred in, with many of them being free tickets given out to local clubs.

I knew this wouldn't be going down well with World Snooker and that was the last year Sky broadcast the Premier League.

While I was working alongside the theatre to help promote our show, we got the chance to do some advertising with Liverpool and Everton Football Club. It was also made clear that if I could get Ronnie to go and visit the training grounds, as a bit of pre-publicity, then we would get lots of local newspaper coverage. I am a massive Liverpool fan so the chance to visit Melwood and rub shoulders with Gerrard and Carragher was a dream come true. The only day that would work was in-between our shows in Ipswich and Bedworth, and the only time slot we could get was 10am.

I checked the map. It was 245 miles, easy four and a half hours. I knew I had no chance of getting Ronnie to get up at 4am and let me drive him to Liverpool to shake a few Scousers' hands; he has no interest in football to start with and even I knew it was a big ask. So I started to give Jimmy the blather about how ticket sales were slow in Liverpool, and we had this great chance to go up to the football grounds to help with the marketing.

He saw straight through me. "If this is about you wanting to kiss Gerrard's arse, then just say so and ask me properly!"

"Ok Jimmy, will you get in a car with me at 4am, let me drive you to Liverpool to the training ground and then let me drive you back to Bedworth for our next show?"

Silence....

"Are you fucking kiddin' me?" he said, then he smiled. "Of course I will..." and so the deal was done. Well, at least part of it. I just had to convince Everton and Liverpool now that it would be Jimmy coming not Ronnie. They weren't keen!

Luckily for us, Brendan Rodgers, the Liverpool manager, was a snooker fan; in fact he had met Jimmy at Chelsea when he was working with José Mourinho. The gig was on, and for once my Snooker Legends show had opened the door for me to meet my footballing heroes. It wasn't lost on me that the enthusiasm I had was similar to when snooker fans come through our doors to meet our players.

Jimmy had no problem getting up. He was waiting for me, and we actually left early. Ok, he did sleep most of the way but fair play to him.

We were due to visit Everton first. To be honest I wasn't that bothered, but the facilities at Finch Farm were amazing, and we got to chat to the boys who had just come back from international duty and were in having a rub down.

David Moyes was charming, liked his snooker and knew John Parrott well; in fact John's sister-in-law is married to Toffee legend Duncan Ferguson who was working on the staff at the time with the reserve team. We gave Moyes a signed cue and got out of there as soon as we could; I wanted as much time at Melwood as possible!

As we entered through the gates into the training facility Jimmy said I went quiet. I thought back to all my heroes who had basically 'come to work' here every day. Emlyn Hughes, King Kenny, John Barnes and of course Stevie G.

As England had been playing overseas the night before I wasn't even sure Gerrard would be in, but the first player we met, Carra, confirmed he was in, and said he'd go tell him we had a cue for him.

We watched them train a bit from their canteen. They had a couple of 8-ball tables but they were in a terrible condition. All the guys came in and we got our photos. We gave Stevie a cue and Jimmy had a game with Carra and Joe Cole, who he knew from Chelsea.

Brendan Rodgers was charming and invited us into his office for a cuppa, with his assistant Colin Pascoe. We gave Brendan a nice piece of memorabilia signed by Ronnie; in return we got a signed ball and Jimmy got a shirt. Stevie was a snooker fan: he'd had a full size in his house but found it too tricky so had a nine-foot table put in instead. Sadly fixtures meant none of the first team would be able to come on the night but it was still a thrill being there. While there Jimmy promised to get them a 9-ball table. I sorted it, and when it did arrive it was a beauty, red cloth with the 'JFT 96' Hillsborough logo on it.

One funny story did occur while we were in the manager's office. I couldn't help but notice all the self-help books on the shelves, and of course the Steve Peters book. It was obvious Brendan was a scholar. He said that he always liked to pass one piece of advice to his players from any top sportsman who visited Melwood. In Jimmy's case he was so impressed with how Jimmy had lost all those major finals with Hendry, yet kept picking himself up and coming back for more.

Brendan asked him how he managed to do that, what his thought process was, his pen and notebook poised for some whirlwind wisdom he could pass onto the Liverpool legends. To be honest, the answer he got wasn't going to rewrite any motivational book soon.

"Jimmy, I'm a huge fan, how did you deal with losing those finals to Hendry?"
Jimmy put his coffee down.

"Well if I'm gonna be honest, Brendan I was pissed for the first two, got battered in the next one, and my arse fell out on the black in the last one...."

Brendan put down the pen and reached for the chocolate digestives. I think it's fair to say no pearls of wisdom were coming his way that day – unless of course, being a Chelsea fan, Jimbo didn't want to reveal his secrets!

Ronnie's flight to China was from Heathrow the morning after our Liverpool show. Django had organized a car for Ronnie but we had organized a night out in Liverpool to end our tour.

First Ronnie said, "I got to fly off straight after the show."

Then it changed to: "I'll stay for an hour or so, we'll get some food."

To then, after the third vodka and orange, him breaking down and saying, "I don't wanna go China, Jase, I can't do it."

I was pretty speechless. The criticism about his walking away from snooker the previous May had all died down, and the positive media were reporting how great it was that he was coming back to play again. They were going to crucify him for this change of heart and I did worry that the Legends Tour would get blamed.

He was suffering with his back: we'd had to get him painkillers during our tour, and I think that was the official reason for his withdrawal as he had been worried about the long flight. I think the truth was he was scared about the flight and what the pressure of his comeback and playing again would do to him. He'd been rushed back before he was ready and the demons were telling him to run away again: it was the easier option for him. Ronnie's dad was with us in Liverpool and like any caring father was telling him to do what he felt was right, to not feel pressured into going to China if he wasn't ready.

We all went out to the Marriott Hotel; it was Les and Bobby's birthday, two guys known to the players on the snooker scene. Tony Knowles was there as well, someone who had worked on some of my shows in 2011.

Tony, Ronnie and I were chatting – actually I lie, because Tony was chatting and we were listening! (John Parrott tells a story of the flight to Australia back in the 1980s when he decided an hour into the twelve-hour trip to Singapore to go and sit alongside Tony for a chat. He asked him one question about rankings and another about the governing body, and he said the next thing he knew he heard the announcement to fasten seatbelts as they were coming in to land. Tony likes a chat that's for sure.)

By this time Ronnie's mind was made up. The car had been cancelled and his room stay extended at the hotel. I knew there would be a backlash the next morning.

With Ronnie still in retirement but playing Legends shows, we were getting some negative publicity, more I think frustration from snooker fans in general, who could not understand that he was ok to play exhibitions with Jimmy but not enter main events.

The deadline for the UK Championship came and went, then he turned down his right to play in the Masters, leaving one final question. Would Ronnie return to Sheffield to defend his World Championship?

With not playing or getting a single ranking point Ronnie was now ranked world number 29, which would have meant that he would have had to win qualifying matches in the Sports Hall to even get to the Crucible.

However, there is a rule that the following season, the holder is automatically seeded 1 for the next World's, or 2 at any other event behind the defending champion. It was a perfect scenario as he really could play when he wanted to.

In January 2013 we met up for some dinner. "If you can get me the right deal, Jase, I'll enter the World's."

He was still with Merlin at the time but they hadn't delivered anything and Ronnie realized that he wasn't quite ready to hang up his cue for good.

We kept it quiet at the time. I only confided in Jimmy White, who had just started work with the ROK Group who were launching a new vodka called Oval.

Ronnie also wanted to get a cue deal. It was complete nonsense that the world champion wasn't endorsing, and therefore earning, from the sale of snooker cues with his name on it.

I found a deal with BCE/Riley, but they wanted a five-year deal and Ronnie couldn't commit to playing for five years. In 2014, he signed the five-year deal with BCE/Riley and his last manager will enjoy the commission from replicating the deal I set up. I won't get anything.

I formulated a plan with Jimmy that if he could get ROK boss Jonathan Kendrick (always known as JK) to a hotel in the West End then I'd get Ronnie there and we'd try to do a deal.

Ronnie had given me a figure he wanted. It was significant and I explained that no one would pay him that amount for one tournament, especially when he hadn't played for twelve months and could get knocked out on Day 1. They might, however, if he committed to play ten events the following season.

On the flip side I was emailing ROK saying that this would be headline news: not only would they get exposure from him playing at the World Championships, where the defending champion always opens proceedings, but also from a news conference I could arrange with BBC, Sky and ITV. I was overplaying the deal for ROK and underplaying it to Ronnie. God knows why, as I had nothing to gain financially.

Jimmy got JK to London and I persuaded Ronnie to come and meet him.

JK's background was motor racing; he had made his fortune as an importer of Yokohama tyres, supplying people like the late Ayrton Senna and Eddie Jordan. His wide ROK Star portfolio of companies included oil, water, security systems, mobile phones, energy drinks, beer and the new vodka.

We stayed about an hour. The deal was done in five minutes with a handshake – the rest of the time was spent discussing their mutual love of motor racing. The deal was easy; keeping the deal quiet and arranging the press conference was not!

We had until February 27th to confirm his entry for the World Championship; we decided to do the press conference on the 26th taking it right to the edge for maximum impact. I started working with a marketing guy at ROK called Bruce. He was great and it was like we were planning a clandestine special forces raid, which, seeing as he was a former tank commander in the army, was quite ironic.

On 5th February we did a Legends event in Ireland, with Ronnie and Steve Davis. Even Steve was asking Ronnie if he was going to play in the World's. Rather than deny it or lie to the Nugget, Ronnie simply said he hadn't decided what he was doing.

We wanted to get a Central London hotel, and we ended up with the Metropole Hilton in Edgware. It wasn't ideal and I was very worried that we wouldn't get the press and I would end up with egg on my face.

In the interim we had paid off Merlin. They earned a significant sum of money from Ronnie for printing off a contract. I thought he could have fought it but he just wanted to take the financial pain and move on. Over the years Ronnie has refurbished a few lawyers' offices with his legal fees and I think it just wears him down.

I got my PR lady, Debbie, on it and we released a statement. I wanted to dangle the carrot but also not give it away. I must had done a dozen different drafts, but in the end it simply said, *"**Current World Snooker Champion Ronnie O'Sullivan has called a press conference on Tuesday 26th February to make a statement to the press and clarify his future career plans.**"*

I'd confided in only one other person, Talksport presenter Andy Goldstein. Andy had hosted Jimmy's testimonial for me and we'd become friends when meeting at the Sky Events. He was snooker mad and even played at the show in Brighton for us as our special guest.

Andy went to school with Ronnie; I think he was a couple of years above him. He does the late show on Talksport, getting in at about 2am. Don't feel sorry for him, he has his dream job!

However, that said, I didn't want to drag him from his home after a few hours' sleep for him to hear Ronnie roll out his "I'm retiring" speech.

The news was going to be confirmed by the first line of my statement. Andy had already typed the tweet and he hit the send button the moment I said it – he was the first to release the news to the sporting world.

We'd got Sky there, BBC and ITV, it was a huge relief. Jimmy was coming as well; he was now a ROK Ambassador.

I picked Ronnie up about 10 am; he was coming in ripped jeans and a shirt. For once I had to advise it wasn't appropriate. He'd packed a pair of black trousers and a jacket and we had to get the team in London to rush out for a waistcoat and white shirt.

I smuggled him into the hotel, and we chilled out in the room so he could change as the world's sports press were assembling downstairs. Ronnie's World Trophy was also making an appearance, alongside the Oval Vodka brand of course which he would soon be wearing.

It was from this day that I took on a short tenure as Ronnie's manager – well, maybe not manager, more organizer. It was a role I probably could have taken on full-time on two other occasions but it was one I shied away from because of my friendship with him.

Commercially earning commissions from him was easy, certainly not rocket science. Companies were coming to him to spend their money but I didn't want to be the guy dealing with any issues or problems with World Snooker, or telling him off for not signing autographs for fans.

I was happy to help out 'unofficially' up to the World's but not beyond that.

Of course history shows that he went on to win the championship so my managerial record with Ronnie remains unequalled: one tournament, one victory, one world championship!

One thing I did miss in the chaos of the press conference was a courtesy call to Barry Hearn and Jason Ferguson. I felt this was important but of all the places in the world you could get a mobile phone service, it seemed the Metropole in Edgware was not one of them. I did get through to them both just after the conference but that was wrong really. They should have been told beforehand.

Of course Barry was ecstatic; the price for the eventual tournament sponsor BetFair probably went up straight after the call!

Very few people thought Ronnie could take a year off the sport and come back and win it. There weren't really any comparisons in sport to judge it on.

Sure, in boxing a fighter may not fight for a year, but he is training and sparring.

Apart from his Legends shows Ronnie had not been playing; his cue was being stored at his mum's. He knew it was a huge challenge, but he also knew he had eight weeks to prepare for it and it was perfect motivation for him.

Ronnie went live on Sky News, Radio 5 Live and ITV. We got loads of tabloid coverage the next day, and part one of the job was done. I felt proud to have got it this far but I wasn't earning a penny from the deal.

I was away working when Ronnie had to go to do the publicity for the World Championship. Barry Hearn was sat there, centre stage; Mark Selby was suited and booted; and Ronnie was in a hoodie looking completely disinterested in it all. It didn't look great to be honest.

The sponsors Betfair had designed a gold cue for any maximum break. They did a photo shoot with Ronnie in his hoodie looking down the cue. It was like a cover for the computer game *Assassin's Creed* – very bizarre.

The build-up to Sheffield was crazy and the pressure was telling on him. I needed to do his logo, and ROK had discussed using a different logo for each session to get publicity for more than just one of the brands.

It was a good idea and actually something Jimmy had been doing for years, although in Jimmy's case he'd had to do it when he sold two logo patches at an event when you could only wear one!

People kept asking if he had a water problem as he seemed to be visiting the toilet after every frame. What they didn't know was it was like Mr Benn in the bog as he switched waistcoats each time – that's Jimmy!

However there was a problem. The world champion only had one waistcoat. Unbelievable, really. Like saying Tiger Woods only has one golf shirt.

Historically the BBC coverage would start at 1pm on the first day and start with a review of the morning's play when the defending champion would begin his campaign. The return of The Rocket meant that BBC were going live at 10am. JK and ROK were delighted: huge viewing figures were guaranteed.

I arrived in Sheffield on the Friday afternoon. Ronnie was at his usual hotel and I went down to get his waistcoat to put the logo on. I caught him coming back from the physio: he'd pulled his hamstring running, not ideal preparation.

I wasn't invited up to his room to collect the waistcoat; he brought it down and then arranged with me to bring it to the Crucible the next morning. It felt a bit strange, and I knew Damien was in town, but I'd assumed I'd be at least spending some time with him. I didn't expect to be sewing on a logo sat in the Hilton Hotel, especially as I was surrounded by Audley Harrison and his entourage who were fighting in Sheffield the following night. Goodness knows what I looked like sat there with my thimble on amongst these pugilists!

I also had some more aggravation around an advertising deal I had done with Programme Master, the company who had the contract to sell space in the official World Championship brochure. I'd been taking a few adverts out across the year with them at the major snooker tournaments, and also took one in the West Ham United programme when we had a gig in Essex. This time they had a great deal: as well as a page in the programme, I could appear in the digital copy on the World Snooker website with a link to my Snooker Legends App, the topic of my advert. I also asked if I could display a pop-up banner in the foyer of the Crucible. The footfall across the seventeen days there is huge and a nice banner advertising my app, which was free to download, would be hitting my target audience. "No problem," said Programme Master; we were a loyal partner.

I guess at this point no one thought to check with the commercial director at World Snooker, the bloke I'd had an uneasy relationship with over the Eurosport issue, to make sure it was ok to have a competitor's brand plonked in the middle of the Crucible concourse during the World Championships. Either that or he missed exactly who this deal had been done with. I duly dropped off my banner on the Friday to a guy called Simon; I just knew that once it went up in full view, someone was not going to be pleased. But I'd done the deal, signed the contract, and paid my money.

I quickly learnt that the World Championship, and the expectation and pressure, brought out a very different side in Ronnie. His best mate Irish Chris had arrived and I got the impression that the inner circle for the World's would be limited to him and Damien Hirst.

There was no real issue, but here I was paying for my own hotel room and fuel to Sheffield. Perhaps Ronnie assumed ROK were paying for it and maybe ROK felt that Ronnie was paying it. Who knows? I never mentioned it.

I walked down to the Crucible with JV that morning; there was a real buzz in the air. Crowds were gathering at the stage door but Ronnie never uses it, preferring to avoid the crowd by diving through the gap in the security fence.

By sheer coincidence as I reached the corner so did Damien's car with Ronnie in it. He saw me and took me through with him. I carried the waistcoat to his dressing room and so started a weird superstition of me always delivering his waistcoat on day 1 of a major.

We did it in Sheffield that year, he won; we did it at the Masters and he won. We also did it at the World's in 2014 and he was runner up – but as Meatloaf says, "Two out of three ain't bad".

After leaving Ronnie to prepare for his opening match with Marcus Campbell I walked round to the front to make sure my banner was up. It wasn't. I chased down Simon and he awkwardly said Miles Pearce, the commercial director, wouldn't let it go up. "Too late," I said, waving the conveniently-placed contract I had in his face. "I've signed a contract. I suggest you take that to Miles and get the banner up straight away."

This was the morning of Ronnie's comeback, and the place was heaving. The banner did eventually go up, but not until after the first day. Maybe Miles felt he had some sort of victory in stopping me advertising on the opening day of the championship. All I know is I had sixteen more days of it up and got all my money back from Programme Master, which in turn meant it didn't get paid out to World Snooker.

Because of work I didn't go for the second round or quarters, but I was back for the semi-final against Judd. Ronnie was getting stronger as each game went on, and people were beginning to believe that he could achieve the impossible.

Judd would be a different proposition to the others; he was the young kid on the block. He'd reached the final in 2011, won a few tournaments and was driving round in a Ferrari. He'd also started wearing shoes that apparently cost £2,000 but made him look like he was treading on a pair of hedgehogs. Once Ronnie got in front he never looked back, and won quite easily.

Judd was dispatched and the opponent for the final was Barry Hawkins. To many the job was done, and beating Barry, who was reaching his first final, would just be a formality. No such thoughts from Ronnie; he was far too experienced to think that.

It had always been a tradition at major finals for his kids, mum and sister to appear for the final session, but there was a problem. Unbeknown to Ronnie, and intentionally kept from him, Maria was pretty unwell. I knew she had been to hospital for tests. It was pretty serious but she was adamant that her son shouldn't know.

She didn't think she would be well enough to attend the final and knew that she'd have to tell her son that morning. Damien had sent his driver to collect Ronnie Junior. With Ronnie well up in the match overnight it was odds on that he was going to win his fourth world title in the most remarkable of circumstances.

I spoke with Maria at about 5pm on day 1 of the final. She wanted to be there but there was no way she could drive. I offered to come and get her. I felt it was important. I lost my mum at just twenty-eight years old; you only get one mum.

That night I drove back home from Sheffield, some 250 miles, to get in at about 1am. At 6am I set out again to Chigwell to collect Maria and her friend Sinead, two hours again. Then we had the three-hour trip to Sheffield itself. I'd done five hours and about 350 miles to get to the Crucible to find that there were only two passes on the door. I gave them to Maria and Sinead.

I did feel a little sorry for myself but Rachel at World Snooker got me a ticket so I was able to watch, although to be truthful I was falling asleep.

Ronnie knew his mum was there but he had no idea how she got there or that she wasn't well. I've never told him.

As we all know, he won the title to create a fairy-tale ending. When he paraded the trophy round he came to the part we were standing in and offered it up. It was a nice touch to think he acknowledged I'd played a very small part in helping it happen.

Without me getting him the ROK deal would he have entered at all? We will never know, but history shows that Ronnie O'Sullivan took a year out of the sport and came back to defend his World Championship. Typical O'Sullivan.

It is generally accepted in the world of snooker that if Ronnie plays to his best then he will win the majority of competitions he enters, especially when matches are over the longer format.

I would think that all his challengers would be looking to see what Ronnie does that gives him that 'edge'. It's not about potting balls: all professionals, and many top amateur and club players, can clear a snooker table, and let's face it, snooker is still an individual sport. It's you against the table.

As far as I am aware, in over a hundred years, the positions of the pockets have never moved, and it's still a bit of wood you hold with a lump of leather on the end of it. I will concede the balls are no longer ivory, but my point is the game hasn't changed. In tennis, for example, how the ball gets hit back across the net from your opponent can influence how you play. In snooker it's you and the table; Ronnie can't make you miss from sitting in his chair.

Ronnie is an elite sportsman. He eats the right things, he trains in the gym and yet even though none of these traits are hidden, it seems unbelievable that none of the other top players try to copy him.

Rory McIlroy said that when he started playing golf he wanted to know everything about Tiger Woods, from his course management right down to what he had for breakfast, when he ate it and which sort of spoon he would use.

I was with Ronnie at the Champion of Champions in 2014 when Ronnie played Marco Fu. At the interval, with Ronnie 4-0 up, he was tucking into fresh smoked salmon with lemon juice, he made sure he got half a litre of water through him during that fifteen minutes to rehydrate him, then topped up on nuts and enjoyed a nice cup of tea chatting to me about how his concentration was. This wasn't him relaxing; this was his match preparation for the second half.

Marco was sat alone in the tournament office. Madness to me that in a tournament carrying a first prize of £100,000, he didn't have some sort of support network with him. He needed someone there to remind him how bloody good a player he is.

I've seen so many players treat the mid-sessions as a time to get on their phones, eat a chocolate bar, grab a cigarette or do their social media. Seriously, do you see Roger Federer tweeting between the change of ends or Lionel Messi posting up a selfie at half time?

Then of course there is the way Ronnie has embraced the mental aspect of the game and his association with Dr Steve Peters.

To my knowledge Steve Peters can't make a twenty break, he has no concept of what a snooker stance or a cue action is, or know what type of tip Ronnie uses, but you ask The Rocket what the most important aspect was of his remarkable win at the World's in 2013 and he will repeatedly refer to the mental coaching of his doctor.

Why aren't all the other top players knocking on Steve's door? Why don't they see the way the best player in the world lives his life and try to learn from it – is it because they are happy with mediocrity? Or are they just too lazy?

There is generally only one first place; I guess it all comes down to how much you are willing to sacrifice to get a shot at it. For the time being it's pretty difficult to shoot higher than a Rocket.

CHAPTER 16

The Legends Cup Year One
Day 1

I don't watch a lot of golf these days, I play even less, but I've always been a huge fan of the Ryder Cup, so when I heard Dennis, Cliff and JP talking about how much they used to enjoy the snooker team events, it got me thinking.

Snooker used to have a team event called the Nations Cup, which was an invitational snooker tournament created in 1999. The event featured teams of four players representing their country against others but it was purely singles with rotating match-ups. It was staged at a time when snooker was really popular and it offered a nice alternative to the regular one-on-one match play, as, to be fair, did the Hoffmeister Doubles! The first winners of the Nations Cup were Wales with a team of Mark Williams, Matthew Stevens, Dominic Dale and Darren Morgan. The event only lasted until 2001.

By 2012 I was already in a position to pretty much stage whatever I wanted. I had all the players on board now, including Ronnie, and I thought it was time to offer up something different for the Legends fans. My issue of course was financing it. By having eight players at an event, the wage bill was going to rise.

I first discussed the idea with JP. He thought it was great and I shared my vision: again four players would represent their countries, like the Nations Cup, but they'd be playing doubles and singles with a point per match. Each of the first three sessions would have two doubles matches and then four singles, with the final session being all singles. Again, does that remind you of anything? Singles were one-frame shootouts but with the doubles I made them best of three. However, if it was 1-1 then we just put the black up for a re-spot instead of playing out the third frame, which would mean there was drama every step of the way.

I also wanted the event to be settled in a dramatic fashion so decided that the winning post should be eighteen points. JP thought that was too much: "Make it fourteen like the Ryder Cup is," he said. He also pointed out that it was pretty tough for one team to get to eighteen when the format I was suggesting only offered up twenty-six in total over the four sessions.

But that was my point. I didn't want a team to get to eighteen in normal play. I wanted to stage a dramatic finish by playing out the twenty-six points and then having all players in the arena facing off with black ball re-spots. It should mean that at the point of victory all the players were out there with the fans, ecstasy in one corner and devastation in the other.

At the end of the day it was still an exhibition with players getting appearance money, but I needed to add an edge. It had to matter, otherwise those emotions I was trying to conjure up would never be real. I owed it to the fans to put on an event where all the players would be trying as hard as they normally would in a ranking tournament.

JP said, "Put a bit of prize money on it to make us try – but not too much so you lose the entertainment feel of your event." It was great advice.

The idea of a Legends Cup was born. Now all I needed was a venue to support it which could minimize my financial risk. After all, just because I thought it was a good idea, and one snooker player did as well, it didn't guarantee it was going to work, did it?

My saviour came by way of an unlikely location but which had a manager who shared my vision. His name was Tim Norton and the venue was Bedworth Civic Hall.

"Where?" you ask. I know it was hardly the Crucible or Wembley Conference Centre but, it was ideal for a number of reasons.

Bedworth is a market town near Nuneaton in the Midlands. It's about twenty miles east of Birmingham, and fifteen miles northeast of Warwick. Nobody could argue it wasn't central.

What Bedworth offered me was a theatre manager who was keen to put his venue on the map for major sporting events. He had tried to get snooker before, and almost got the Sky Premier League, but the hall was a few feet too small for the camera runs.

Because the council had shared this vision they were prepared to guarantee me a fee for bringing the Legends Cup to their venue, plus we had a local hotel, Weston Hall, who would provide free accommodation for the players. It was a huge project but because of the support from Nuneaton Council it was relatively low financial risk for me.

I wanted to work with the players who were already in the team. I felt loyal to them, and so I needed to take some artistic license with the teams.

My captains were going to be Dennis and Cliff, two foes from as early as 1973 when they first played each other. I knew they would take it seriously, and beating each other as captain of their teams would mean as much as beating each other in a major ranking final.

I also needed to include Jimmy, Ronnie and JP, so a team of England and Northern Ireland was created. It was in theory the UK without Wales and Scotland – I'd already created my own devolution far in advance of what Alex Salmond tried to do in 2014!

Thinking about Cliff as captain of the other team, I knew it couldn't just be drawn from Canada. At the end of the day Cliff was sixty-five years old, a pensioner, but still their best player. The opposition needed to be competitive as the England and Northern Ireland team had the current World Snooker Champion, Ronnie, on it.

I wanted to use Stephen Hendry as well, so the easiest thing was to call the team the 'Rest of the World', then I could also draft in Ken Doherty from Ireland and Tony Drago from Malta.

Once the selections were announced many argued that Cliff's team was far stronger than Dennis's and would win comfortably. The fact it was generating debate amongst snooker fans was a good sign for me.

I've always admired how the Ryder Cup is able to get weeks of mileage and publicity out of what is really just a three day event. The viewing figures on Sky for the opening ceremony itself usually compare well with coverage of a top Premier League football match; they are masters of exploiting their brand commercially. The clever thing that adds extra interest to the Ryder Cup opening ceremony is that until that point the golfers do not know who they will be playing against. The captains announce their line ups live on TV in front of a global audience. It's dramatic and I thought to myself, "I'm nicking that".

So before the first day's play we also decided to stage a Launch Dinner where the two captains would announce their pairings, and playing order. Not only that, a player from each side would play a match for the first point. This meant that as well as a dinner, and the speeches, the fans could see some snooker as well. It was limited to 150 people but it sold out really quickly just like the Higgins show in 2010. I'd undersold it!

Ticket sales up to the event itself were ok, but not spectacular. Then of course, just five days before the Legends Cup, Mr Ronnie O'Sullivan went and won the World Snooker Championship for the fourth time. That certainly helped.

Sadly Ronnie was knackered after the championships and didn't want to come to the dinner. I was a little upset but also worried how people would react. All the other players were there and there had already been Chinese whispers amongst fans about him not showing up for the weekend after his exploits in Sheffield. A few of the players had asked me too. The guy had just won £250,000 for becoming world champion; did he really want to roll up to Bedworth five days later for another weekend for a few grand, after being away from home for three weeks? Would you?

Worse of all Ronnie wasn't the best at keeping in contact and would go silent for days, not answering his calls. I didn't have any reason to think he wouldn't show up but when everyone kept asking me over and over again, I'll admit now, the doubt crept in.

This was the biggest show we had every done. Basically it was five of our normal shows over-packed into three days. I needed The Rocket.

The Launch Dinner went well. For snooker fans, having access to so many stars in one room was like being in a sweet shop. The soup and chicken supreme were passable – no one complained as far as I know.

For the snooker at the dinner I'd asked Jimmy to represent England and Northern Ireland, and Tony Drago to play for the Rest for the World. I felt having captains Dennis and Cliff grind out a best of three could have seen us there till midnight!

Jimmy won a close match and Team England went 1-0 up. The captains made their speeches and announced their line-ups. Ronnie was first match on, partnering Dennis the next morning... but I had no idea where he was or if he was coming.

I went to my room about 11.30pm, just as the guys started a game of poker. While they were all having great fun and playing Texas Hold 'em, I felt a headache coming on. It was undoubtedly 'Rocket fever'.

After not sleeping a great deal, I got the call at about 9am. "Jase, it's Ronnie.

I'll be with you in about two hours."

It was a great relief but the minibus was leaving Weston Hall for the venue at 11. I bet my life he wouldn't be dressed ready to play.

Everyone was in high spirits and the friendly banter had started. Confirmation of Ronnie arriving just topped it off.

Drago was sore at losing to Jimmy: he was the unofficial mascot for Cliff's team, full of high fives and hugs – I'm not sure what Stephen Hendry really made of it. As a man who had accomplished so much as an individual, in a largely individual sport, the idea of being part of a team wasn't something that came easy.

By 11am Drago had doubled up on breakfast and was into his second Mars Bar, adrenalin and a sugar high making for an explosive combination for the Tornado. Cliff was doing his Tony impression, and when they all clambered onto the bus, it was like a 'jolly boys outing'. All we needed was a singsong and a 'kiss me quick' hat.

Ronnie arrived about ten past eleven. The bus had gone, and he had his dad with him. "All right Jase, traffic was a bit bad; can we get a bit of brekkie?"

"Brekkie?" I thought. "We start the show in an hour and I need you down the venue."

"Full English, no mushrooms, mug of tea!" barked his dad, and the chef got to work.

It was nearer half past eleven before we left but the two Ronnies, junior and senior, had enjoyed their grub and the mood seemed ok.

Ronnie's dad informed me he wanted a pass so he could go wherever he wanted to, and that he also had some guests turning up so he wanted VIP tickets for them; they needed to be looked after. It felt a bit forceful, but I've learnt that this is just his way. He only has one volume setting, and it tends to be on full most times.

I think Ronnie's dad was enjoying the chance to attend an event with his son. Because of what happened in the past, he doesn't show up at major tournaments. He probably feels it would be an unfair distraction for Ronnie and added pressure. We've always got on ok; we've had our moments, but he knows I always do what's best for his son, and that makes me all right by him.

England and Northern Ireland started well and led at the end of Day 1. To the delight of the crowd Ronnie had made a century.

In the players' room we showed the action as it happened on a big screen and

Drago was bouncing off the walls, getting so involved. It was nice to see it meant so much to him and his enthusiasm was infectious and spread round them all.

The score at the end of Day 1 was 9-4 in England's favour. Ronnie hadn't lost a game, Drago was pissed at his team's performance and Jimmy was giving it to him big time.

"What's the score, Tone?" said the Whirlwind.

"Did you win today?" was another.

Drago wasn't happy; it was a day for some serious comfort eating. Luckily in that department he couldn't be defeated.

We got the bus back to Weston Hall and the idea was we'd enjoy a Chinese meal and have a few drinks!

A few drinks.

Did I mention we'd have a few drinks?

I had a few drinks, Stephen had a few drinks, and Dennis had a few drinks... Ronnie... drank the equivalent of a bottle and a half of vodka, with orange of course – got to keep up the Vitamin C!

The last thing I witnessed, as I went to bed about 2am, was Ronnie sat on Hendry's lap licking his ear and telling him how much he loved him.

"You're the guvnor you are, the best, the bollocks. When I was young I wanted whatever you had, didn't I, Dad? I wanted the same trainers you wore, the same jacket, didn't I, Dad?"

Hendry was very patient about it, and it was quite amusing to see eleven world titles crammed into one armchair.

Here was a man having a blow-out after seventeen days of immense pressure in Sheffield. I didn't begrudge him that; I just wished he hadn't chosen to do it at my event.

Ronnie was chain-smoking, in the bar of a non-smoking hotel. "It's ok, it's Ronnie," they said. "He can do whatever he likes."

The irony of the similarities to how Alex Higgins once flaunted authority and rules wasn't lost on Cliff Thorburn. "Let's hope he doesn't shit in the wardrobe like Alex did once," Cliff said

"Fat chance of him even making it upstairs to his wardrobe," I thought to myself.

CHAPTER 17
The Legends Cup Year One
Day 2

At about 2am I extracted myself from the party and went to bed. It had been a long day, and part of me felt that by sleeping I didn't need to worry about what may be happening downstairs. I was physically and mentally exhausted. Surely, I thought, tomorrow will be less stressful?

I set my alarm and closed my eyes, desperate for rest. I glanced up at the smoke alarm above my bed. The little red flashing LED light was reassuring. At least I'd know soon enough if a stray reefer had set fire to the hotel.

When I got up at about 8am and went down to breakfast it was obvious that Ronnie wasn't going to be troubling the maid today. He was still up, his bed not slept in!

Ronnie and referee Jan Verhaas had done an all-nighter – quite impressive if you don't have to go pot balls for a thousand people in a few hours. Remarkably Jan seemed ok. They make them tough in the Netherlands, I thought; either that, or he was a bloody good actor.

Ronnie was still in his blue playing shirt. JV's daughter Brooke-Leah had stayed up too, but she had obviously stopped drinking many hours before and was trying to get him in some sort of order. Everyone was stunned by the state of him.

"I can't play Jase, I'm ruined."

For once words failed me.

I said to his mate 'Scouse John', "Get him in the shower quick. He's playing in two hours."

John felt guilty; he'd been up as well. Ronnie's dad wasn't happy either; he knew it was unprofessional and blamed John.

Somehow we got Ronnie into a shower; I made sure it was cold! We dressed him and helped him onto the bus. I slapped some sunglasses on him and I just hoped we'd be able to get away with it because the crowds had gathered outside the stage door on Day 1.

"I'm only playing because it's you Jase," he slurred. "Anyone else and I'd have stayed in bed today. Only cos it's you."

I think I was meant to feel grateful. Maybe I was. Any sort of Ronnie was better than not having Ronnie at all.

I kept telling myself it would be ok. The other guys were saying how sorry they felt for me. They were all running in the other direction from this situation though, wanting no part of it!

It was time to stick together. We collectively had to get this Rocket safely back on the ground, because trust me, at this particular time he was flying and way out of control. The England Team was leading 9-4 but their prize asset was in another orbit.

Session 3 Part 1

ENGLAND AND N.I. 9 REST OF THE WORLD 4

The first match of the third session was doubles and it was Ronnie's turn to partner Jimmy – the partnership the fans had been waiting for, and one Dennis had been saving up to use. They were up against Stephen and Tony Drago. Tony knew how important it was to get off to a good start for Cliff, trailing as they were, so he was probably the only one secretly delighted at the state the World Champion was in.

First, before any play, we had the VIP reception, a chance for the people who had paid around £60 to sit in the best seats, meet all the players and have a glass of champagne.

On Day 1, at the previous two VIP receptions Ronnie had reluctantly walked in carrying the World Trophy. The crowd loved it, he didn't. He was also, of course, the last name announced and got the biggest cheer; he was our top of the bill.

Today, Ronnie could hardly stand, but when his name was called to enter the VIP room he waddled in carrying the World Trophy between his legs like it was his cock.

Everyone laughed. 'It was just Ronnie being Ronnie.' I swear that weekend he could have walked on water. He was titanium.

JP said, "I wonder what Joe Davis would have made of that."

We all laughed as it broke the tension. We paraded him round the VIPs and then got him into his dressing room. Time was going to be the only cure for this hangover, but time was the one thing I didn't have.

We discussed moving his match to second on, but Jimmy quite rightly pointed out that if we got him through the doubles, he would have a couple of hours to get his head down before a singles encounter. Ironically that was against Stephen Hendry, the man whose ear he had been licking a few hours earlier.

People had been buzzing about their match-up from the night before when it was announced; within the camp we assumed Stephen wouldn't have too much trouble against a misfiring Rocket!

I was relying on Jimmy, Stephen and Tony to get Ronnie through this. England won the toss and Ronnie decided to break. For some reason he decided to try a break-off shot where he would place the cue ball between green and brown but hit it diagonally through the blue and pink to catch the reds on the opposite side. It's not even a break you would use in exhibitions.

Everyone could see he was still pissed; he slumped in the booth and leaned on Jimmy's shoulders, falling asleep at one point. I look back on it now and laugh – even Ronnie does – but at the time it was really stressful.

I was praying that either Stephen or Tony would get in quick and clear up. Cliff thought he was guaranteed a point. Ronnie had about two shots in the first frame, one a foul when he went for the blue instead of a red. There was an uneasy murmur in the audience, JV doing his best not to draw attention to the fact Ronnie was sozzled.

Jimmy, being Jimmy, got in and made seventy and won the first frame on his own. ROS had a kip. Drago was mortified.

To everyone's amazement, halfway through the second frame, with the scores roughly level, Ronnie made the best drunk forty-eight break you will ever see: six reds and six blacks. Behind the scenes we were speechless; I think the three other players were too.

9-4 became 10-4 and England won the next doubles as well. It was turning into a rout. The score was 11-4 going into the third session singles.

The Rest of the World Team were in trouble. To have any chance going into the final session they had to get three out of the four remaining points in the singles. The victory total was eighteen, and Dennis and co. were already bearing down on it.

Fresh cakes arrived from the local bakery in the interval. Jimmy said, "Better get one before Tony sees them", but the Tornado was nowhere to be seen and neither were any other members of his team.

Cliff had taken them off together for a little chat in the dressing room, a call to arms to basically pull their fingers out. Again, I think Stephen felt it was all getting a bit too serious.

Session 3 Part 2

Fate decided that first up in the singles was Ronnie v Stephen. A clash of the titans, a four-time world champion with the world's biggest hangover against a seven-time world champion with a Thorburn rallying speech ringing in his ears.

Stephen won and sparked a comeback. Tony, Cliff and Ken all won their singles. From 11-4 it was now 11-8. As a Liverpool football fan it felt a bit like Istanbul in 2005 when they came back from 3-0 down to win the Champions League. JV was pumping up the crowd. It was game on again with everything to play for going into the final session.

Final Session Part 1

There were eight points on offer in this session, and Dennis needed seven of them or we were going to re-spots and sudden death. The draw came out.

Dennis went with strength in the first half. Ronnie, Jimmy, JP, then himself. Cliff put Stephen on, then Tony, Ken, and left himself to face off with Dennis.

Ronnie was now feeling better and dominated Hendry to turn over the result from the afternoon's match. It became 12-8.

Jimmy followed on by beating Tony. It seemed like the revival from the afternoon was over for the Rest of the World: now 13-8. But this wasn't over, and Ken and Cliff grinded out victories to make it 13-10 into the final session.

Final Session Part 2

Jimmy went out first to play Stephen; it was a Crucible rematch. Being three points behind, Cliff needed Hendry to pile more misery on Jimmy. Stephen responded, as champions do, and hit a 120 clearance. The break would go on to be the highest of the tournament.

Stephen had just made the last eight of the world championships and hit a '147' maximum break on the way. He may have been retired but he was still sharp. There was no way he wanted to play second fiddle to anyone.

13-11, within two points again...

Next up: Ronnie v Drago. Tony had his chances, but I think, if anything, he was trying too hard and Ronnie nicked the frame. 14-11 now and within four points. JP took them a step closer beating Cliff, but then Ken turned Dennis over, so that at the end of normal play the score was 15-12. It was Sudden Death time.

Sudden Death – Black Ball Re-Spots

Each captain could nominate who to represent their team but they had to go through the entire team before anyone could shoot twice. Suddenly momentum swung and the first four black ball re-spots were all won by the Rest of the World.

Tony Drago was screaming. I feared he could have an aneurism but the crowds loved it. The England and Northern Ireland team had gone quiet; JV was running out of superlatives. Remarkably the Rest of the World now led 16-15 and were just two points from victory.

Dennis went to the Whirlwind, to face Tony. It was tense. Four safety shots were exchanged before Jimmy was left with a half-chance. He nailed it, the crowd went wild, and even Ronnie was hugging him. 16-16.

Ronnie was up next. Everyone was smiling but inside, no one wanted to be the person who let the team down. Ken played a bad shot: adrenalin meant he over-hit the black by about four feet. Ronnie faced a tricky black across the nap... By now table etiquette had gone out of the window and there was banter flying from both teams. Ronnie held his nerve and potted it. England and Northern Ireland were once more in control at 17-16.

Fate almost decreed that with just one point needed for victory, and that victory possible with the potting of a final black ball, that Captain Dennis Taylor would step up for his Team. Cliff had to win this point or the fight back would have been in vain.

Cliff played a dump shot to the side cushion; Dennis had a double on, a 'barney rubble' as we call it. Would he go for it? Of course he would. For once there was no time for a gag, no telling any stories about his brother Seamus (he never had a brother called Seamus by the way). This was tense.

Standing where he was, Dennis knew the ball was in before anyone else. His team went mad. They had won the Legends Cup!

JP performed his own 'Dennis 1985' finger wag and everyone embraced. Ken, Stephen and Cliff smiled and congratulated the team, and so did Tony, but the Tornado was hurting.

Victory speeches were made, confetti fired, and although one team had beaten the other, everyone had played their part in putting on a fantastic event. As Ronnie left, still not trusted to drive, he said to me, "You're a clever c**t with them black ball finishes, Jase."

It's not a quote I can often repeat out loud, and people say the funniest of things when they are pissed, but it meant a lot.

CHAPTER 18

2012 Tour

2012 was a pivotal year for Snooker Legends. As well as the first staging of the Legends Cup we also played shows in Ireland, Jersey, Preston, Radlett, Stoke, Telford and Ipswich. We also played a show at the Fairfield Halls in Croydon. It was a 'Ronnie night' and The Rocket was firing on all cylinders, making our tour's third maximum 147 break.

Eighteen centuries were made in total that year, again not a bad return over twelve shows.

However, I felt a bit like Alex Ferguson: I had to break up the original team. It was hard to do emotionally but I knew it was a correct commercial decision. I'd based the first two years largely on the same four players, but with the addition of Hendry, Davis and O'Sullivan I was now spoilt for choice, and the casualties from regular shows became JP and Cliff.

JP also lost his horse-racing contract with the BBC at the same time, as the sport's coverage moved onto Channel 4, so it was a double blow for him. I'm sure John wasn't reliant on the Legends for income but I know how much he enjoyed them. He still does a few shows a year for me but nothing like the fifty he did in the first two years. JP will say it gives him more time on the golf course!

With Cliff it was more a financial decision, as return flights from Toronto aren't cheap, plus of course he has to have accommodation during all the downtime in-between shows. Again The Grinder's appearances are sporadic now, but I am desperately trying to take the Legends Tour to Canada where he can then be a mainstay. Twice we've been close to finding sponsors to fund it and twice it's fallen through. I do feel for him, as I know how much he loves being involved in the game.

I'm involved in a new coaching program called SightRight that I've made sure Cliff is the ambassador for in Canada. I hope when that takes off we can work together more again. More about that later.

It's fair to say in 2012 my first choice line up for a four-man show was now Jimmy, Dennis, Steve Davis and Stephen. Within a few shows of putting them together, Stephen and Steve formed this new double act. It was like Peter Kay and Victor Meldrew – Davis was Kay! Steve is without doubt, as I have mentioned before, the best exhibition player I have ever seen, and Stephen has a naturally dry sense of humour. They dovetail so well. In the other pairing it's much simpler: Jimmy pots the balls and Dennis tells the gags. With JV and Michaela it's a tried and tested formula.

I never put Ronnie in a four-man line up. I did it once in Berlin and it didn't work. No disrespect to the other players, but if you put him on the bill, then people want to see him playing all the time, not sat in the dressing room while others play.

Generally on a two-man show it's Ronnie and Jimmy. They sell the most tickets, so commercially it makes sense. Sometimes I will use Stephen and Jimmy: their Crucible history makes it a good story to base the night on, and I bill the match-ups as 'Crucible Memories'. In 2015 it will be twenty-five years since Stephen first won his first world championship, so we are planning some nights to commemorate that. Jimmy will probably enjoy the work more than the event itself!

Stephen's first show for me was one such 'Crucible Memories' show in 2012 and it was appropriately at the Crucible Theatre itself. We did a short video for the crowd about their clashes there, and it went down so well, we show it every time they play each other. Jimmy always makes a point of not watching it.

It seems as if the current World Snooker contracts are going to prevent Jimmy playing in our Crucible shows until he retires. That's a shame in my opinion, and an example of where I think some discretion and common sense from the governing body should be used.

CHAPTER 19

2013 and the Deal with Eurosport

At the start of 2013 the only place you could see Ronnie O'Sullivan play snooker was on the Legends Tour. Looking back it was a position I could have exploited more than I did. Perhaps it was commercial madness to get him the ROK deal to return to snooker, but I always felt playing a major part in that would pay me back further down the line.

We travelled to Goffs in Ireland in February and I staged Ronnie and Steve Davis. I also took Dennis in the commentary role instead of JV.

Not having Jimmy around was weird to start with, but to also not have the reassuring presence of JV made it feel like a different show. However I was still aware that we needed to keep evolving, and JV and Jimmy had played three shows there already. With the exception of The Rocket, audience numbers will naturally drop the second time you return to the same venue unless you freshen up the line-up.

With Ronnie on the bill it sold out, of course, and he played beautifully while fending off the numerous questions about him returning for the World Championships.

For a few months, up to Sheffield, my own tour took a backseat to the 'assistant manager's' role I was doing for him.

It had been announced that he was due, and contracted, to play in my Legends show in Sheffield that April, but once World Snooker realised the implications of me having the world champion in the Crucible when they couldn't get him I had Barry on the phone.

This time I was in a position of strength and I had to ask myself what Barry would have done if the roles had been reversed. In a game of poker I had the winning hand; how much was I prepared to bluff it up?

The issue was I knew Ronnie *was* going to enter the World Championships but the deal with ROK included an embargo on disclosing it. Once that did come out then Ronnie would have to sign the player's contract which would have meant appearing for me in Sheffield at the same time as the qualifying was on for the main championships would have put him in breach.

Throughout the call I tried to hint as best I could the reason why I agreed to replace Ronnie in return for permission to use Davis and Jimmy. I truly think Barry just thought I was being helpful, which I guess I was in some respects.

I was averting a huge PR disaster for World Snooker, but also I'd been staging this particular show for years. The conflict with the player's contract occurred when they started trying to commercialize and charge spectators for the qualifiers at the English Institute of Sport down the road.

What I had done during this time was punt my product out to all the major broadcasters. Without Ronnie, their ratings were dropping: Sky had already decided they were going to cut right back on snooker.

All the major broadcasters responded, except Sky, and I got meetings with BT Sport and ITV. Every time, though, the same thing came up: they either already had existing contracts with Matchroom Sport, Barry's company, or an existing relationship with Barry himself that they valued.

The only other snooker to date, aside from Barry, had been something called Power Snooker, a form of snooker that was notable for two things

1: People couldn't understand the rules, even the referees!

2: It became acceptable, in fact encouraged, to shout out to players, resulting in particularly harsh personal abuse of Shaun Murphy.

Ronnie had been paid a lot of money to front it. The guys behind the project were good theatre producers and they'd got some money via boxing promoter Frank Warren. The ballpark figure banded about was that they lost about £250,000 on the first show at the O2, and then they staged it in Birmingham and lost a similar amount.

Throw as much money as you like at something, but if the issue is that the fans and players don't like it, how will it ever grow?

Why didn't it work? Well who am I to say or criticise, but the cloth they chose to play it on was so fast it could make the players look silly, and you did need a degree in maths to keep up to date with the scoring. Double points for this, triple points in a power play, ball in hand... Quite frankly, it was messy.

I know they are still trying to resurrect the idea of Power Snooker. In some ways I wished they had come to me with their financial backing, as we could have done great things with Legends and Ronnie at that time.

Out of the blue I got a call from Eurosport. Behind the scenes, and unknown to me, they had been contemplating trying my events for some time – no doubt the Ronnie ratings factor again. The Legends Cup gave them something different and guaranteed them the big names.

There were a number of issues, namely getting the World Snooker sanction I referred to earlier, but also, as I had an unproven product, I had to commit to raising an awful lot of money towards the production costs.

I took a punt and said I could do it. The wheels were set in motion. I didn't have a sponsor, but when Eurosport started putting pressure on World Snooker to grant my sanction then suddenly I became a threat.

I was, in theory, moving from staging nice little exhibitions in theatres in the UK to a global TV audience which could in theory cannibalize theirs. I understood the risks, but I was a big boy and I felt that getting a TV broadcast had to be the next step for the brand.

Having just helped secure the sponsorship deal for Ronnie to return to the sport, ROK, the 'Oval vodka' company, as I called them, seemed an obvious choice to approach as a partner.

I laid out a full presentation to JK and his team, and explained we could brand the event not only with his vodka but with his beer company too. The potential reach for Eurosport was huge but French law meant that we couldn't call the event after one of the alcoholic brands. JK's parent company was called ROK Stars and so the ROK Stars Legends Cup was created, with one team wearing the Oval Vodka logos and the other wearing the ABK Bavarian Beer logos.

The company wouldn't pay up front though. It was a risk and maybe not one I would have taken had my personal circumstances not recently changed.

I had had responsibilities but now I didn't. I had been living with my partner and her four children in a large house in Essex. When the Legends Tour began, it was never my intention to tour with every show. I hadn't been 'on the road', so to speak, for ten years as a touring actor, and realistically being away from home so much wasn't part of the plan.

After Sheffield and Higgins it became clear to all that I had to be at every show.

This wasn't something that could run itself or be trusted to an assistant. The strain of doing fifty away trips in two years took a toll on my personal life and the relationship broke down. I moved into rented accommodation and really shred myself of all my commitments and responsibilities; it was because of this that I was able to take a gamble with this production. I only had myself to worry about.

All of a sudden it became very real. I had my sanction. I had my broadcast. Snooker Legends was going to be live with a potential reach of 132 million people in thirty-two countries. I took a moment to thank Peter Ebdon and Grame Dott for giving me the idea in the first place.

However running a normal event and running a live TV event were two completely different things. Add to that, the nature of our event meant that players were changing over after each frame, a logistical nightmare when you literally have the commercial break to get it sorted.

We did venue visits and decided we'd go back to Bedworth. I felt good about that; they'd finally got a chance to put the venue on the map. Live TV was coming. Tickets were slow: was it punters' lethargy after seeing the event last year, or did the fact you could sit at home and watch this event from the comfort of your armchair mean people didn't want to attend in person?

I know from being a football fan that nowadays I'd rather watch the action at home on Sky than pay high ticket prices to sit in the cold at the ground, staring at ants running around half a mile away.

For the second year of the Legends Cup the line-up was almost the same as year one, with just one change to each team. Steve Davis was going to play for England and Northern Ireland, and world number one Neil Robertson was going to join the Rest of the World.

JP and Ken were the two players who got replaced. I felt bad and a bit disloyal, but getting Steve Davis to play, a six times world champion, was a no-brainer, and Neil was from Australia, world ranked number one, and of course the 2010 world champion.

Ronnie did his trick again and won the World's and this time he attended our launch dinner! I'm not sure how much the fact that the event sponsor was also his tour sponsor had to do with it but everyone was glad he was there. However this time I couldn't get in contact with Neil Robertson; if it wasn't one thing it was the other.

I'd only met Neil briefly once when we were at the Masters promoting Jimmy's testimonial. He seemed ok and we worked direct. He had a reputation for being pretty disorganized. He was late to a couple of Premier League matches, and obviously needed a proper manager.

About a month before the event I met a guy called Mukesh at the World's. Muke, as he was known, had been Mark Selby's manager for a few years and had done very well out of it. Then I think Mark met Vikki, Muke met his wife, and things got a bit complicated. They split just before the World's and Muke said he'd started managing Neil.

Ok, I thought, it kind of made sense but I immediately got the impression that any agreement they had made had got somehow lost in translation. I truly believe Muke thought he was managing Neil, but I don't think Neil thought it was an official arrangement.

Anyway, I got a call just before the event from Muke asking for tickets for the launch dinner. No problem, as Neil's manager it's a courtesy I am happy to extend. However it all became a bit farcical when Neil went AWOL on the day and his new 'manager' obviously didn't have a clue where he was or what he was up to. I was pretty pissed. I had the pressure of Eurosport, I was entertaining my sponsors, but once again a top player was missing. I felt that, instead of enjoying my hospitality at the launch dinner, Muke should have been in his car down the A14, tracking down his client and dragging his arse to Bedworth as he was contracted to be at the event.

Neil had perforated his eardrum so there was a legitimate excuse, but his communication was poor, and initially it didn't give me a good impression of him. Fortunately when he did arrive the next morning he was a dream all weekend, and he's someone I like and always chat to at events. He's got himself a good manager now, but sadly that management has priced him out of working at current Legends events. I hope that changes in time as he is a hell of a player and one of the few who can stand toe-to-toe with Ronnie.

We got the news that the first afternoon would be a delayed broadcast ,with us going live in the evening. That did give us a chance to ease ourselves into the event. I was going to act as tournament director, which meant wearing a headset and being in constant communication with the broadcast director. I blagged that it was fine. I may have seemed in control but I was nervous. Sometimes running a Legends show is more about managing what's going on away from the table than just on it.

Ronnie wasn't a fan of us having TV at our events; he feels it takes the fun out of it. I do know what he means, and having done it, I accept having the brand on TV isn't the be-all-and-end-all, but it does give you huge global exposure for your product.

At the launch dinner it was Jimmy and Tony who faced off for the second year running. The result was the same, and Team England and Northern Ireland went into Day 1 leading by one point. I took to my bed at Weston Hall knowing that although The Rocket was safely tucked up we were about to go global. What on Earth had I created...?

CHAPTER 20
Eurosport Legends Cup, 12.3 Million

Day 1 Session 1

ENGLAND AND N.I. 1 **REST OF THE WORLD** 0

Going into Day 1 Cliff was very aware that he couldn't let his opponents get a good start and lead like they did the year before. He knew that Dennis liked to load his draw top-heavy but in Neil Robertson he felt he had someone who could take Ronnie on, and try to neutralize his scoring power.

The first match-up of doubles saw Dennis and Ronnie beat Stephen and Neil, but then Cliff and a real in-form Tony turned over Jimmy and Steve. Honours even.

Even at this stage I had a feeling the matches were going to be very even. The event was coming across well to the TV guys, with plenty of humour. The biggest compliment I could pay JV is that Eurosport decided to mute all their own commentators while the frames were on and simply let JV run the show. They only top and tailed, and took us in and out of commercial breaks. I think it was being translated into five or six languages.

Going into the singles we were still waiting for our first century. Ronnie played beautifully to make 78 and beat Stephen, but Neil hit straight back for Cliff and beat Steve, blow for blow. Jimmy was in with 106 against Cliff, then

Drago muscled Dennis out of a frame and celebrated like he had already won the Cup. The first session ended at three each, with only the point from the night before giving Dennis a slight advantage.

The players were also playing for two individual prizes: the £1,000 high break as normal, but also a newly created 'MVP', most valuable player. Again it was something I had unashamedly stolen from the NFL in America but it was another responsibility I bestowed on JV.

The prize wasn't bad either: a Swarovski crystal clad bottle of Oval vodka, estimated worth £5,000. It was worth winning, and of course it was full of premium structured vodka.

We went back to the hotel for a break, just in time to see the afternoon's play get broadcast on TV. It was a great moment and I shared it with my mate, Michaela. She had been there from the very start, the very first show.

My phone started bleeping. People were watching, comments were nice. I felt good. It all seemed worthwhile.

Back on the bus, and session two was ready to break off.

Day 1 Session 2

ENGLAND AND N.I. **4**   REST OF THE WORLD **3**

As this event was a bit different, Eurosport were encouraging JV to have chats with the players in the arena. They then decided they'd like to do some interviews in the players' room – see how the players were feeling, and get their views on the match.

I was the only one who could do those interviews, and in truth I think they knew the best chance they had of getting Ronnie on camera was if I asked him. The interview I did with him also included Michaela. Here they were having a laugh and a joke with each other, but only five or six days earlier, Michaela had to discipline Ronnie for a 'cue wanking' gesture he made in his semi-final match with Judd at the World's. It was pretty serious at the time, and on reflection Michaela was right to do it, even though Ronnie claimed he was cleaning his cue. But no grudges were held on either side; here they were making each other tea and chatting like best of mates.

Cliff put Hendry and Drago out in the first doubles; they were up against Ronnie and Steve. Of all the players, Ronnie looks up to Steve Davis. While many kids were Alex Higgins or Jimmy White fans, for Ronnie there was only one guvnor, the Nugget. Ronnie still has a picture of him getting Steve's signature when he was eleven years old.

Drago dominated the first frame. His fist was pumping and he was exuberant, but this match was a best of three. Much as Drago tried to get Hendry involved in the emotion of it, Stephen really found it tough to let go. He'd hardly smiled when he won his world titles; he was hardly going to cry like Gazza at an exhibition.

Frame 2 and Drago went in with 52, in under two minutes. He was literally running round the table. It was very entertaining but, as so often in Tony's career, he missed a simple ball and let Ronnie in. Ronnie cleared beautifully with 65 and then potted the re-spotted black; it was first blood to Dennis again. Tony looked devastated; the mood back in the players' room was not great. I ordered the girls to restock the chocolate bowl!

Cliff and Neil hit straight back for the Rest of the World but again it took a great 63 from Robertson to nick it; the doubles were shared.

Ronnie won the first singles against Neil, but Stephen hit back with a break of eighty. His opponent on the end of the drubbing was of course Jimmy. Tony beat Dennis, and then Steve beat Cliff, so overnight it was 7-6.

"Let's have some Chinese," Ronnie said. The colour must have drained from my face as I was transported back twelve months. He laughed.

"Don't worry Jase, I ain't drinking tonight. Wanna do a run in the morning."

Ronnie did drink but it was the odd glass of wine and he was in bed before me. Feedback had come in from Eurosport: it was going well.

However, the Legends event girls were starting to get some social media abuse. They'd been used as walk-on girls and had been part of the team for years, known to all of the players. Photos had appeared before of them with the guys, but now it seemed some fans were jealous. Both Georgie and Michelle posted pictures of themselves with Ronnie and Stephen, and 'slut', 'slag', 'whore' were all words that followed. It was unacceptable, and another downside to getting the brand on TV.

Day 2 Session 3

ENGLAND AND N.I. 7 REST OF THE WORLD 6

Jimmy and a perfectly sober Ronnie went out first and battered Tony and Neil. Ronnie made 117; it would be the highest break of the tournament. The same tit for tat continued with neither team able to break away.

By the end of session three, the scores were 10-9, the only highlight of the singles being a hundred from Hendry, his second of the tournament.

Day 2 Session 4

ENGLAND AND N.I. 10 REST OF THE WORLD 9

Both teams needed to get to eighteen; Rest of the World had never led but had never trailed by more than one point either. The all-important singles were upon us.

I'm not sure what Cliff said, but suddenly they caught fire. They won the first four singles matches. Neil beat Ronnie, his first defeat of the tournament; an inspired Tony beat Jimmy; Stephen beat Steve; and Cliff grinded Dennis. Suddenly it was 13-10 and Cliff could sniff victory.

Dennis went to Jimmy to stop the rot; it didn't work. Robertson was flying and a 90 made it 14-10. Relief came as the Rocket defeated Hendry, and Dennis was inspired and defeated Tony. 14-12 with one singles match to go. It was a repeat of the 1983 World Final: the Nugget Steve Davis against the Grinder Cliff Thorburn.

It was no secret that in their playing days these two didn't get on. It would be easy to say it was all Steve, but I don't think Cliff ever thought he consistently got the better of Steve, which can make you grumpy. In this frame Cliff lived up to his catchphrase, 'every shot was a pint of blood'. He won and took his team to within three points at 15-12.

Sudden Death – Black Ball Re-Spots

ENGLAND AND N.I. 12 REST OF THE WORLD 15

Just twelve months earlier the scores had been reversed. Dennis still had a chance. First up were Drago and Jimmy. Drago nailed it for 16-12 and celebrated like it was over. Even his team mates laughed at his reaction. It was electric in the arena, and I could only hope that it was translating that way on the screen at home.

Cliff up next against Steve, and the Nugget played a good up and down shot leaving the black only a few inches off the top cushion. Cliff eyed up the cut. Surely he had to play safe? If anyone would play safe it would be Cliff, wouldn't it?

Not a chance. Cliff cut the black in; Robertson jumped up at the same time as Drago and almost knocked Tony out with the butt of his cue. No one noticed until Tony sat covering his eye. It was chaos. The Rest of the World were within one point of taking the Legends Cup. Dennis turned to Ronnie.

Ronnie played a great shot, Neil replied, they went back and forth. Ronnie knowing that he couldn't afford to leave Neil a half-chance to pot it. Ronnie caught a safety too thick and the ball headed diagonally down the table. It seemed as if everything went into slow motion as it headed for the pocket. In truth this wasn't how I wanted it to end: in any penalty shoot-out you want the winner to be scored, not victory gifted by the opponent missing.

Neil theatrically pretended to blow the ball towards the pocket. There was no need: the cloth was so fast the ending was inevitable. The cue ball dropped in, the Cup was won, Drago was bouncing, and Ronnie genuinely looked gutted.

Cliff took the trophy and made a speech which will stay with me forever. Here was a man who had won everything the game has had to offer, and in the midst of a victory in a team exhibition he stopped to pay tribute to me live on TV. "Jason, mate, we did it. God bless you man."

The cameras did a close up on me, looking like a cock in my headset. I looked knackered, and the camera didn't lie, although of course it did add ten pounds, right?

The MVP was won by Tony; he promptly took the £5,000 bottle of vodka and emptied it down the toilet. "I don't drink," he said.

Jimmy shook his head in disbelief. Yes, the value was in the bottle, but £50 of premium vodka had been thrown away – but that's Tony.

It was an amazing event. The theatricals and nature of Drago got me thinking about another idea. I wanted to make a fly-on-the-wall documentary about him. Even that night in the bar, when I should have been enjoying a beer, my mind was already onto my next project – and it was going to involve a little trip to Malta.

CHAPTER 21

2014 Season, All Change.

When the ratings came through from Eurosport we'd achieved viewing figures of 12.3 million, which was staggering. Of course you have to put it in context, but when you consider that more people watched the Legends Cup across Europe than watched an episode of *The X-Factor* in the UK, I was pretty chuffed.

Our ratings were better than those reported for most PTCs. I couldn't help thinking this was the start of an extended run of TV broadcasts where I would actually get paid for the product I had created. Sadly, I was wrong.

On two separate occasions I got a letter of intent from Eurosport regarding a new broadcast. I even sat with the big bosses in Paris to discuss resurrecting and producing the World Trick Shot Championship for them. It always came down to money. They were getting offered sport for free: figure skating was one example that was always used against me: "Why should we pay for snooker when we get figure skating for free?"

I didn't understand the comparison then and I don't now, save a joke about a few players skating on thin ice.

One person who did like what we did was JK, Chairman at the ROK Group, and in the words of Victor Kiam from the old Remington adverts, "He liked it so much he brought the company!"

Within a month or so of the Legends Cup I accepted an offer to sell half of the Snooker Legends brand to 'Events that ROK' and took up the CEO's position with a stakeholding in that company. It was a massive move for me but one which I felt would finally give me the resources to expand and try out new ideas.

JK invests in people. He loved the idea of having someone like me on board to develop both of our ideas.

Within a few weeks I had Ronnie, Jimmy, Michaela and a film crew in a barn just outside Telford trying out my first idea: 6 Red Pool.

I'd been aware of feedback from America that a frame of snooker took just too long to make an impact with the audiences there. They loved the skill of snooker but not the time it took – hence why you'll never see cricket played much over the pond.

Basically, 6 Red Pool was snooker with six reds played on an American 9 ball table with 9-ball sized balls. It was quick but also had skill. The maximum break was 75 and the idea was to play matches over longer formats, for example first to twenty racks.

Jimmy liked it, or certainly liked the idea of the extra work it could bring in. Ronnie wasn't so sure. JK at ROK loved the idea and the format was put forward for consideration for a TV show in America called *Billion Dollar Brand*. Basically this was a version of the UK's *Dragons Den* but hosted by a billionaire called John Paul DeJoria – who just happened to be a shareholder in ROK Stars. John Paul had already created two billion-dollar brands – Paul Mitchell Haircare and Patron Tequila – and the programme was about his search for a third.

We did the promotional video, Michaela helped write the rules, and I tried out the game at my local club. It was quick, neat, and kids liked it.

I was due to go to America in December 2013 to film for *Billion Dollar Brand*. However, it never happened and 6 Red Pool sits protected, ready for the day when we may get the backing to try it out. Will it ever happen? I'd like to think so but I don't know. It was frustrating to say the least.

Two things that were going ahead were the Drago documentary and the creation of the Snooker Legends App.

ROK had the skilled personnel and track record of building apps for mobile devices. The idea was that if we couldn't broadcast our events we would stream them via pay-per-view into our own app.

I already had a lot of content, hours of previous Legends shows. We could launch the app with a free download; we could then earn revenues from selling 'in app' purchases and our pay-per-view events. I also had hundreds of event photos. It was a project that wasn't going to take much of my time, and any money it brought in was a bonus.

One thing that was going to test my patience was the documentary with

Tony. It was going to be a small set-up, me, Tony and one cameraman called Stewart. Stewart headed up ROK TV at the time so it was all in-house. Tony has a heart of gold but he has a short temper and can be obnoxious and rude. This makes him great value to watch but not the best to work with.

We did our first filming at a Players Tour Championship event in Doncaster. World Snooker granted us access and we spent a few hours interviewing Tony and following him about while he played his first round. I was surprised at how passionately he spoke about his career. Here was a kid from Malta who had left home at eighteen to come and live in England to play snooker. Straightaway he was homesick; he remains so to this day.

The idea was we would do a couple of days in Doncaster but then we'd all go to Malta and film him there to find out where his snooker career began. I was producer, editor and interviewer, and we titled the project from one of Tony's quotes when describing himself, "Fun and torture at the same time". I loved it.

Tony was good value and I knew how to press the right buttons so we could get the full range of emotions: anger at being ripped-off by a manager when he was young, tears when he talked about his mother, and frustration when your scampi and chips turn up thirty seconds before his!

A couple of times he became impatient and took his microphone off. Stewart and I had a signal to carry on filming anyway. So much of the footage that was taken when he didn't think he was being filmed was better than when he was 'acting', so to speak, but the bleep machine was working overtime. We knew he hated flying so we smuggled the camera on as hand luggage so we could witness him at take-off. His suffering and anxiety made great TV!

It was obvious he was loved in Malta; everyone we met on the streets of Valetta hugged him. The reunion with his mother was especially emotional, and I knew if I kept asking the right questions he would eventually cry.

I think the documentary was quite cathartic for Tony as well. By speaking in depth for the first time about his childhood he really opened up. I also think it made him sad that a career of twenty-five years as one of Malta's top sportsmen had still left him needing to earn money to find each month's rent.

Tony has never been married, and to my knowledge never had a long-term girlfriend; his two loves are his mother and food. Looking at early pictures of Tony he was as thin as a rake; loneliness in those early years in the UK was comforted with over-eating.

He was good company and we got great footage. I also interviewed Jimmy

White and pool player Raj Hundal for the programme. We finished the filming at the 2014 Legends Cup and shortly after that it was released on our app.

The response was good; we were only charging 99p for it. Then it got picked up by TVM1 in Malta, the equivalent of the BBC over here. We made a few quid, Tony made a few quid; happy days.

Show-wise in 2013 we had another great night in Belfast. Ronnie was on the bill, and they signed autographs for nearly two hours. We also welcomed 1986 World Champion Joe Johnson to the team in Plymouth, and made him bring the pink shoes he was famous for wearing the year he won. We also returned to Liverpool for a show, and ITV came along and filmed part of Jimmy's *Sports Life Stories* programme at the event.

At the start of 2014 we did a run of shows before the Masters tournament. Ronnie played in Southend, another sell out, but his Legends appearances were now being restricted by his new manager, a bloke who had been put in place by Ronnie's dad with no previous experience.

When this guy first started with Ronnie he badgered me constantly for information and contacts. Daily phone calls asking how to do this, how is this done, do you know this person? I obliged because I thought I was helping Ronnie then suddenly when it came to booking Ronnie for shows this guy increased Ronnie's appearance fees by 300%. Thanks very much: when will I ever learn?

It meant that for much of this time I concentrated on shows with my staple four: Jimmy, Hendry, Davis and Taylor – a proven quartet who always delivered entertainment and were no trouble.

For our annual visit to the Crucible in April I was restricted to only using non-contracted players so once again I couldn't book Jimmy or Steve. I had Stephen of course, and used JP again, his first visit since 2011. I also took Tony Knowles and Joe Johnson back there. The show sold ok but it wasn't sold out; there is no doubt the line-up was missing a Jimmy, Davis or Ronnie.

However for this showcase event I'd introduced a 'VVIP', which was one step up from the VIP we did! In truth I made it up. The players laughed at my guile but this package included a backstage tour of the Crucible with a Legend and a chance to play on the table with Stephen. They also got their photo with the World Trophy. Add in the overnight hotel and I sold the twenty slots easily. Stephen was wondering what I would come up with next! My mate Andy came up to the Crucible and won the raffle to play that night – people said it was fixed but I had nothing to do with it. I actually own a snooker club in Newbury with

Andy and a guy called Lyndon called...The Crucible.

I'd tried plenty of different merchandise lines; again some of the random items I used to sell had the legends shaking their heads in disbelief, or was it admiration? Cuff links, mouse mats, coasters and my particular favourites... fridge magnets! We also did iPhone covers: we sold them, but I quickly realised that Apple changed their phone designs too often to make it viable.

I decided to stream the Crucible Event live into the app. We did it for free to try it out and as I had no contracted players, World Snooker couldn't stop me doing it. This was more about testing the technology ready for the streaming of our Legends Cup which was taking place a month later.

Another guest, and a way of selling more tickets, was a seven year old lad I'd seen at an exhibition with Jimmy. Young Westley Cooper from Leicester wasn't tall enough to reach the table, so he stood on a box that he trailed behind him. I say it was a box, but it was actually a bread tray. It was hilarious, but this kid was talented and I reckon in about ten years I'll be selling that footage to the BBC when he plays in the main championships. It started out as a one-frame challenge match against Stephen, then Stephen potted a ball and got booed; he said it felt like he was back playing Jimmy again!

Snooker Legends had given one young boy the chance to play in the Crucible. That could never have happened before our shows and it's moments like that, and taking the former players back there, that makes it all worthwhile.

Another ace up my sleeve was that for the 2014 World Championships Ronnie went out wearing my logo, the Snooker Legends App. We got thirty thousand downloads – it was perfect advertising. Just as the Eurosport broadcast was a big moment, so was this. The defending World Snooker champion, and world's most popular player, was going out live on the BBC wearing my brand.

We almost had the fairy tale ending as well, and I truly believe one black ball off the spot at 10-6 up cost Ronnie the title. But fair play to Mark Selby, never has the World Championship been won by someone who battled for it, or indeed wanted it, more.

For the 2014 Legends Cup I decided to announce new captains and it was Dennis and Cliff who had to make way. Jimmy would captain England and his nemesis Stephen the Rest of the World.

Steve Davis and Ronnie were givens for Jimmy's team but I took a punt and booked the ladies World Snooker Champion, Reanne Evans. I knew she could play, and commercially I thought it was a good move. I was also frustrated that she was largely unrecognized in the game and I think had got lost with a previous management who had twenty-plus players to look after, most of whom were delivering more commission than she was.

For Stephen's team I booked Drago – his MVP performance a year earlier made that an easy one – then I went for Mark Williams from Wales and a controversial selection, Dechawat Poomjeang from Thailand. 'The Poom', as he was known, was a madcap player who had made a real name for himself at the previous world championships with his antics.

People loved him but I got criticised on social media. "He's not a legend," they said. I had to remind them that he was in fact a former World Amateur Champion and a superstar in Thailand. We were streaming worldwide so I thought I could capitalize on that.

I got my World Snooker sanction; again, as I met all the criteria, they couldn't really turn me down. We were charging £2.99 for the whole two days' stream booked upfront or £4.99 if you booked on the day.

I also left Bedworth behind and went to a new venue, The Hexagon Theatre in Reading. It was one I had used before, and it has a history of staging tournaments. We'd done well before with shows there and I'd been working with the venue since 1997, but once again sales were slow, despite me having eight players with thirty world titles between them.

Then to top it off there was a military coup in Thailand which prevented 'The Poom' getting his visa to come to the UK. Not for the first time, I had player problems just twenty-four hours before the event. I got on the phone to Ken Doherty; he got on a plane at short notice and answered the call for the Rest of the World.

Looking at the teams, I once again found it difficult to decide who I thought would win. Sure, England had the world champion in Ronnie, but analysing the other three, Steve had fallen off-tour, Jimmy had just clung onto his tour place, and Reanne had never beaten a top pro in a ranking tournament.

For the Rest of the World you could argue Stephen would be rusty, but in Mark and Ken you still had two top performers, and with the way Drago approached these tournaments, I made them favourite.

How wrong I was. Jimmy's team dished out the biggest hiding I have ever seen. In the first match both Jimmy and Reanne had century breaks, Reanne's a beautiful 117 clearance where she took the final blue left-handed, the pink right-handed and the black one-handed. She made an immediate impression, and playing in front of a big crowd seemed to inspire her. The only player to show any fight for Stephen's team was Mark Williams, who weighed in with two centuries himself.

The match was over by the start of the fourth session: England had won 18-3. We played out the matches as a courtesy to the fans that were there but we never got any black ball finishes. Reanne won the MVP award; as well as her centuries, she was undefeated in the doubles, and had also beaten Drago and Ken in singles matches. Ronnie didn't drop a frame all tournament and made the tournament high break, a 133.

We did have Eurosport with us, but only to film an episode of *The Ronnie O'Sullivan Show*. I gave them full access to everything in return for a pledge that Ronnie would interview Reanne. By now I'd reached a deal with her to take over her management and my search for tour sponsorship for her had begun.

That summer we took the show to the Isle of Man and also Inverness in Scotland. I could sense it was becoming harder to sell tickets. In some ways my reliance on Ronnie for full houses was becoming greater than ever.

In September Ronnie asked me to find him a proper management to start developing his global profile and prepare for a career when he no longer plays tournament snooker. It seems he had finally seen what most of us had realized months earlier, namely that the choice he had made with his current manager was a huge mistake. All this guy had done was go round telling everyone how great he was, when in truth he knew fuck-all about snooker. He claimed to be this hugely successful businessman, but I later found out he ran an electronic cigarette shop in Walthamstow!

After one show, he came up to me to congratulate me on the tickets sold, but then informed me that I had to change the cloth, since in his opinion it just wasn't right for Ronnie to play on the one we were using. I said I would give him three guesses to tell me what cloth we were actually using that night and if he got it right I'd change it. He soon shut up.

He then asked me to approach Ronnie's former manager, Django, to see if he wanted to sell the Grove Academy where Ronnie still practised. Looking back, I can't believe I did it, but he told me Ronnie was aware of the idea and it didn't make sense for Ronnie to be practising in a venue owned by his former manager. The truth was he was jealous and insecure that Ronnie would go back to Django. A few months later I had to smooth it over with Django. He must have thought I was a right prick for trying to buy his Academy when I now lived over a hundred miles from it. Ronnie had no idea.

This guy also had the idea of creating a new website and then charging fans to join it. It was complete madness. By offering them a signed photo and exclusive access to blogs and online chats, something Ronnie was never going to do, he felt he could charge people £19.99. Some people did sign up and the new management are now in the process of having to try to refund people and manage the negative feedback from those fans who handed over money but never got their goods. Needless to say a new website, that doesn't charge fans, is under development.

Back in 2005 I wrote the stage show for a children's TV programme called *Engie Benjy*. The two main characters were voiced by Ant and Dec and they agreed to record the stage show for me. This brought me into contact with their managers, who were called James Grant. Now James Grant isn't a person but it was the middle names of the agency's founders, Russ Lindsay and Peter Powell – yes, he of Radio 1 DJ fame.

At this time they were a fairly small agency; now they are London's largest and still look after Ant and Dec, as well as stars like Keith Lemon, Philip Schofield, Davina McCall and people from sport like Neil Warnock, Clint Dempsey and England cricketer Jonny Bairstow. I thought they would be perfect for Ronnie and so called up my contact from that time, a lady called Ali Astall, who became Dec's fiancée in 2014.

I took Ronnie in for two meetings with James Grant; they weren't desperate to grab him and that was actually a good thing for him. They only wanted to work with him if they felt they could make a difference, and they were aware of a reputation Ronnie had for not turning up to tournaments.

I did a lot of work behind the scenes with them and met them on more than one occasion on my own. I was convinced they were right for him, plus of course it meant he would get rid of the previous manager. Ronnie signed and I became, for the short term, the 'snooker advisor' to James Grant. I was back travelling with Ronnie to tournaments and at the first one I returned for, the Champion of Champions in Coventry, Ronnie won and walked away with a cheque for £100,000.

I quickly was able to book new shows with Ronnie and start concentrating on my next big project, the Irish Legends Cup. A tournament that would pitch Ireland v England in Dublin? Fair to say that would get the juices flowing.

During this season it was decided that World Snooker would no longer run any Player Tour Championship Events in the UK. These events are regarded more as the second tier but they do attract a lot of the top amateurs. I decided to create my own style of PTC, and so the Snooker Legends Pro-Am Series was born.

I could stage it at my own club. The idea was to get sixty-four amateurs to play on the Saturday down to sixteen qualifiers and then invite sixteen pros to join them on the Sunday. It meant that club amateurs could win two matches and get a dream tie against a pro, with twenty-one points a frame start.

I lined up my sixteen pros. I was able to get Jimmy, Stuart Bingham and Tony Drago easily and then of course could add in Reanne and a few other pros I had met like Michael Wasley and Barry Pinches. I was delighted when fellow pros Mark Davis, Rob Milkins, Ben Woollaston and Jimmy Robertson contacted me. The event was a great success, and from a networking point of view I got to meet many of the top amateurs too.

It was won by Daniel Wells, who carried off £1,200, and we had ten centuries in the weekend. Amateurs really enjoyed getting to hang out with the professionals and we did a few Crucible Burgers that day too! A few local amateurs took a pro scalp as well: those club tables certainly a leveller.

The Pro-Am series is something else that I will develop further. At the time of writing this, we've already staged our second event, this time won by Mark King, and a third one is currently being planned.

I've never been more involved in snooker and yet I've never actually played less than I do now. I am thinking of giving it a go again in one of these Pro-Am Series events. The middle of the white can't be too hard to find again after all this time... can it?

CHAPTER 22

The Irish Legends Cup

After three years of keeping the Legends Cup the same, and, if I am going to be honest, prompted by low ticket sales in Reading, I decided to rework the event and stage the next one in Ireland.

The venue was easy: the horse sales ring in County Kildare, known as Goffs. Back in the 1980s and 1990s Goffs was the home for the Benson and Hedges Irish Masters, and it is a venue quite like no other, with the table sitting in a tight circular area with the crowd in close all the way round. With steep seating the atmosphere was electric there, as was the legendary hospitality. Benson and Hedges piled lots of money into the event. It was hard for a member of the general public to get seats as they were mostly gifted to the corporate partners of Phillip Morris, the brand owners.

For Bensons, the snooker was really a sideshow; the hospitality enjoyed by the chairman of someone like Tesco's ensured that orders were placed for millions of cigarettes over that week for the following year. I'm not sure you'd get away with it nowadays but getting your quota of product into these outlets was big business and well worth the cost of staging the tournament. Also, of course, any player who played in the tournament left there with a lorry load of fags, a gift from the sponsor. Players were encouraged to smoke; if you could associate your brand with someone like Jimmy White or Alex Higgins then that had a real value for them... until of course the next tournament when a new sponsor like Rothmans or Embassy were handing out the cigs! In the 1980s plenty of top sixteen players always had some cheap smokes for sale if you had the readies at hand.

Nowadays once a player loses, he is in his car and down the motorway as quickly as he can; for the Irish Masters Tournament you had to stay till the end irrespective of when you got beaten. Finals were staged with many of the other top players in their evening suits sitting in the front row for the cameras, there as a guest of Mr Asda or Mr Morrison. It was all about the image.

I first took snooker back to Goffs in 2011. When it's full of snooker fans it truly is a remarkable place to be. If I needed to stoke up the atmosphere any more then why not pitch Ireland against England? It had only been nine hundred years since the Norman Invasion and let's not forget the involvement of the Earl of Kildare, titled after the county we were staging the match in.

After he demolished Stephen's team in Reading, Jimmy wanted to captain England again and take the same team to Ireland. Steve Davis and Reanne committed immediately, but Ronnie wanted to see what access he was getting to his kids over Christmas. That was understandable as the event fell between Christmas and New Year; I was sympathetic to his priorities but still disappointed.

I turned to Ali Carter. If ever there was an inspirational English snooker player to replace The Rocket it was going to be him. First he had coped with Chrohn's Disease, then he had testicular cancer, the same as Jimmy, and he'd only just returned from a form of lung cancer to play again. I knew that the Irish fans would welcome him with open arms, even though he was on the opposing team: they love and admire a true battler.

For Ireland I decided to go the way of the old Nations Cup and pull from both Northern Ireland and Eire. So in reality it was All Ireland.

Ken Doherty was captain, a former world champion, and with the nickname the 'Darlin' of Dublin' it was an obvious choice. Ken also has other nicknames, 'Crafty Ken' is one and 'Careful Ken' is another. I'm not sure if the 'Careful' Ken is in any way related to the story where shortly after his 1997 World Championship Victory, where he pocketed a cool £210,000, he rewarded his car with a new set of remoulded tyres!

I brought back Dennis Taylor – after Alex Higgins, he is Northern Ireland's most decorated player – and then I was stuck with choosing from a possible three other candidates for the two remaining berths.

Fergal O'Brien is the only player who has ever phoned me and almost begged to be included; in fact, I probably could have got him to play for nothing! Being a local lad, within a stone's throw of Goffs, he was desperate to represent his country; he also pledged to work hard to sell tickets for me. Fergal was in, and with hindsight never had I made a better decision.

So it came down to a choice between Mark Allen and Joe Swail. Rankings-wise it was a no brainer; Mark is regarded as one of the top ten players in the world and a multiple event winner. Joe has been around for a while, so certainly qualifies for Legends status, and people forget he has made two semi-finals at the Crucible.

The fly in the ointment, and one that clouded my judgement was a little girl called Lauren. Lauren is the daughter of Reanne Evans and Mark Allen, and it's a broken relationship. Being Reanne's manager meant there was an emotional involvement.

However the devil in me, the event maker, thought that having Mark on the Ireland Team and Reanne on the England Team would be electric. Nothing sells better than controversy.

I spoke to Reanne and told her that commercially I should be booking Mark and that we'd exchanged messages on Twitter, and he was up for playing. Michaela also said that he was excellent in exhibitions with people, another quality we look for on these shows.

Reanne said she wouldn't have felt comfortable him being there, so I stayed loyal to her and did a deal with Joe. It was the right decision to make as the manager of Reanne; it was probably the wrong decision to make commercially for Snooker Legends and the event.

The Launch Dinner was being taken out of my hands. I'd sold it to a colleague of Ken's who had booked the Mansion House in Dublin and was going to stage a charity event. I knew the amount I usually made for the dinner, which was money that went towards the prize money and hotel costs at the event. Of course I could never guarantee I would make that much, so selling the event was an easy decision.

I started getting nervous about the event in October when the guy wasn't coming back to me with final details. Also I was offering to help him sell tickets so found it strange he wasn't engaging. All the players' flights and hotels had been booked around arriving on Sunday 28th and attending the event that night.

When he finally did get in touch, he admitted he'd paid a 5k deposit for the Mansion house on the Saturday not the Sunday, and was struggling to sell tables. He blamed Ken for saying the Saturday, and I got the impression Ken was more involved than I had initially thought.

I always incentivise all the guys to earn if they bring sponsors to the table so Ken was on a commission for delivering this. I'm not sure if he was earning a bit the other end as well. Either way, it was a mess and the guy had to cancel the dinner. It seemed as if problems with the Legends Cup just seemed to crop up wherever I staged it.

Staging a three-day event is a major operation; staging it in another country makes it costly and logistically tricky. I was nervous that without Ronnie the event could struggle to sell enough tickets to cover costs. I thought staging it so close after Christmas would mean we'd sell lots of tickets as presents. In the lead-up to the event I almost dreaded getting the reports from Ticketmaster – with a month to go the sales were woefully short of my break-even point.

I'm old and ugly enough to know putting on any event is a risk. I'd been burnt badly in Reading in the May but I'd like to think not one player ever knew exactly the trouble I got into – £50,000 worth of trouble. Selling the tickets and promoting the event is my job. I don't treat the event or players any differently if I am making or losing money. You will never hear me go to a player after an event and ask him to take a smaller fee because I have lost money; that's not my style. Then again I don't go opening the chequebook to offer them extra when I've made it either, so it works both ways.

As I said earlier the thing I admire about Barry Hearn, and something he tells me is mutual, is that we've both put our hands in our pockets and risked personal money. It takes balls to do that. As my good friend Neil tells me, "Sometimes it works and sometimes it doesn't. The key is not to feel either way about it."

By the first week of December tickets started to pick up, I was selling twenty to thirty a day. Fergal O'Brien must have sold me near on a hundred tickets easy; he worked so hard to promote the event. In some ways if all the other guys showed the same commitment to making the event a success as he did, I could sit back stress-free. Fergal, you'll do for me on any future event like this in Ireland.

The launch of Jimmy's second autobiography meant he had a promotional trip to Dublin two weeks before our show; it was a perfect chance to join him and turn it into a PR event for the Legends Cup as well. We caught the red-eye flight out of Heathrow and by 8am we were sat having breakfast in Bewleys Hotel in Dublin doing his first interview. We probably did ten to twelve interviews that day, plus a book signing in Eason's.

Jimmy was superb. We laughed at how twenty years ago he'd have never made that flight or had the patience to sit answering the same questions over and over again. At every interview he would plug the Legends; we also met up with Ken and did a great interview for his radio station that had come on board as a partner. We went to RTE and bumped into Nicky Byrne from Westlife. Everyone loved Jimmy; truthfully, I'm not even sure he understands why.

As is customary with every Legends Cup we've done, there was a last minute player drama. At the first Legends Cup Ronnie was drunk, at the second Neil missed the dinner, and at the third 'The Poom', Dechawat Poomjeang, was stuck in Thailand while a military coup went on... This time my mate Michaela was ill.

I was getting nervous leading up to Goffs because she was still off sick with World Snooker. On the 9th December I had no choice but to send the following email to her:

Hi Michaela,

I hope you are well. I've put off sending this email as you know I think the world of you but I need to ask if you think you are going to be well enough to referee at Legends Cup in Goffs in a few weeks. I notice I haven't had your contract back, in truth I'd missed checking for it as we've worked together for so long. I'm aware you haven't been at World Snooker events and the reason is none of my business but I hope you understand I need to make sure I don't get left with only Trish.

If you feel you can't attend, for whatever reason, can you let me know so I can approach Jan. I'm sorry to have to send this email but I hope you understand why

Jason x

I felt bad about sending the email but I knew she would understand. After me she cares more about the Snooker Legends brand than anyone else.

She did eventually phone me to tell me she wasn't well enough to come; I was gutted that my mate wouldn't be with us in Ireland.

Once I knew, we turned to Jan VerHaas, who had worked at the previous few Legends Cups and was one of the team. He'd fit in perfectly. Jan was the referee for Ronnie's record tenth maximum break in 2010 at the World Open. After finding out that there was no special prize for completing a 147, Ron shook hands with opponent Mark King after potting the last pink. Jan, however, persuaded the Rocket to pot the last black and finish his break. Ronnie and

Jan get on well and all through that break Ronnie was muttering to Jan that he wasn't going to pot the final black!

Jan had recently got married to a lady from Belarus called Alena. Jan would have loved to do it but Alena's passport meant she couldn't travel into Ireland. It was their first married Christmas together; I couldn't expect him to leave her.

I talked to Michaela about who we could use instead. Patricia Murphy was already there, and had experience of Legends, but she hadn't officiated at the top level for years, as she'd almost retired to bring up her young family. Michaela was adamant I needed an A band referee, but I quickly learned it wasn't going to be the guy who had officiated at this year's World Championship Final, Brendan Moore.

I've always got on with Brendan. We shake hands at tournaments when I am with Ronnie and always have a chat. To me he would have been the next person to approach and also a recognisable face for the fans in Ireland. Michaela didn't want me to use him. I know Brendan had rapidly risen up the ranks and actually took charge of two of the three major finals last year; he'd also taken on an assessor's role with World Snooker and perhaps sees himself as one day replacing Mike Ganley as the main tournament director.

I don't have any problem with anyone showing ambition. I think Michaela had a problem with him being a 'team player'. Suddenly Michaela wasn't asked to referee the World Pool Masters, the first time in seventeen years she hadn't been used by Matchroom Sport who run the event, and of course own World Snooker – her replacement Brendan Moore, a snooker referee who despite never officiating 9 ball pool was thrust into a major Sky Sports event. I know Michaela was very upset Brendon hadn't got in touch with her before it was announced he was refereeing the Masters.

As I said, personally I have no problem with Brendan, but Legends is all about being a team. Michaela's choice was Belgian Olivier Marteel, a top class referee who took charge of the PTC Finals but hadn't yet got a major final. Within the space of a couple of emails the deal was done and we had booked Olivier.

Again Michaela was right: it was a great choice. Olivier added calm when the crowd got going, and trust me, as you will read later, they certainly got going! He was a joy to work with; nothing was too much trouble and I think he had a great time. I'm now blessed with four great referees on my team; I hope being involved with Legends helps raise Olivier's profile too.

We all arrived in Dublin on the 27th December, via one of the worst ferry crossings you can imagine! We had a long set-up day at the venue whilst the players descended on the town of Naas from all over Europe. Instead of the Launch Dinner we did our own dinner where the wine flowed, everyone relaxed, and the captains announced their line-ups for the first day.

Jimmy put himself and Steve out first and they got paired against Ken and Fergal. That meant Reanne and Ali played Joe and Dennis. In the singles Ali was to play Ken, Jimmy against Fergal, Reanne vs. Dennis and Steve battling Joe.

The English boys got straight into Dennis: "No one wants to lose to a girl!" they jibed. Reanne wasn't bothered; after all she was the one saying it to him! The banter and winds-up had well and truly begun. It was game on!

CHAPTER 23

The Battle of Kildare

Over the breakfast table on Day 1 the talk was all about which team would win. On paper Ireland had three players ranked in the top sixty-four – England only had two – plus of course they were playing at home. Ken had described the Goffs crowd as his Fifth Man but the reality is, Jimmy is loved as much in Ireland as any of the lads who'd be going out in the green shirts. It was a close call for sure.

Jimmy said the key would be how his team performed in the singles matches. Doubles are always a lottery, and quite often the strongest player on paper can easily be shut out. Then, of course, the format I'd created meant that if a doubles match went one frame-all then it was settled with a black ball re-spot, which is a complete lottery.

We had a good crowd in – not spectacular, but it was Monday afternoon and quite a few people had already started back at work. I could sense the new players didn't really know what to expect: was this an exhibition or was it serious? My only advice was it needed to be entertaining – that was the thing that had set us apart from anyone else and every player needed to buy into it and play their part.

There were six points on offer in the first session. Jimmy wanted three, convinced that Ireland would come out strong.

The Whirlwind had purposely put himself in the first match. He got a huge reception and led by example, slamming in a quickfire 63 break to take the first frame. Fergal responded in frame 2 with 65. We were already into our first black ball shootout of the competition and it was only two o'clock!

Before the match Team Ireland had been at the table working out how to play the re-spots. It was their opinion that the top cushion would 'square up' so attempting a long treble was preferable to a double.

As so often in his career Jimmy ripped up the rule book and promptly doubled the black in. First blood to England. If the new lads didn't know what the Legends Cup was all about before, they certainly did now.

Ali Carter got a great reception when he came down for match two and responded with a 73, three frames and three single visit breaks – the standard was high. The second frame was scrappy, but Reanne made some important balls and it was a simple victory for them. 2-0.

It was clear that Joe and Dennis hadn't yet got their arms going, but Ken reassured them that it was going to be a long two days and everyone would play their part.

Into the singles: Ken was playing England's top ranked player, Ali Carter, and you had to favour the man from Essex. Captain Ken fired in a fantastic 107. It would end up being the highest break of the tournament but more importantly it was 2-1. Ireland were on the board. Then Jimmy got himself 34 up with one red left on the table, but Fergal cleared with 35 and celebrated like he'd already won the Cup. The crowd loved it, Fergal was pumped and Ireland were back level.

Dennis did get beat by 'the girl' in the next match but he wasn't guilty of playing badly. The truth is Reanne was just too good. Jimmy had his three points; anything from the last match from the Nugget was going to be a bonus.

Despite being ranked so much lower than Joe, Steve was much more used to playing in front of a big crowd. He won and Jimmy's England had a 4-2 lead. Reanne and Steve were undefeated.

During the break Dennis and Joe were out at the practice table. Joe confided he was nervous explaining he hadn't played in front of such a big crowd for quite some time. It was something I hadn't really considered but so much snooker is played nowadays in front of one man and his dog. Then again Joe had played in two Crucible semi-finals; it's amazing how they can quickly forget how to perform under pressure.

In-between sessions we all dined on roast beef and chicken, and I'm pretty sure it tasted better if you were wearing the blue shirt of England.

Day 1 Session 2

ENGLAND 4 ALL IRELAND 2

The evening's doubles started with Fergal and Joe taking on Jimmy and Ali. Once again this was a key match for Ireland, and they didn't want to drop three points behind in this race to eighteen.

Ali Carter made 50 in the first frame, and an Irish victory looked unlikely. Suddenly 'The Outlaw' Joe Swail got in the balls and ran a beautiful 82 break; it was just what he needed to settle him down. Once again we had a re-spotted black, with Ken watching from the balcony urging the boys on.

After about three attempts Joe was left with a long black and Olivier called for hush. Joe seemed to cue up for ages but his technique held strong and he made the ball. The crowd cheered, but more importantly the score was back to 3-2 and Joe Swail could relax. He'd made his first significant contribution to the team.

The next doubles match with Steve, Reanne, Ken and Dennis had just the eighteen world titles on show; it was the 1997 Darlin' of Dublin who took the frame with an 88 break.

Steve Davis responded and cleared the colours to make it 1-1 and the old black ball was put up again. This time it was Ken who doubled it. He celebrated by calling for more noise from the crowd. He wasn't disappointed. 4-4.

When we started the singles, Fergal beat Jimmy, then Ali beat Joe. The match between Reanne and Ken looked on paper that it should go Ken's way but it was the Ladies World Champion who won it. Jimmy was thrilled: she had won her second singles match of the day.

Ali was looking tired and asked to go back to the hotel. I always knew two long days were going to be tough for him. Sure, he was elated at being given the all-clear only a week before Christmas, but the effects of months of chemotherapy meant he was far from fighting fit. Jimmy jumped in the taxi too; I think he was more hanging from the night before than actually tired!

The final match of Day 1 was a repeat of the 1985 final. We hadn't rigged the draw in any way but it was a great match-up. Steve and Dennis have replayed that frame so many times in exhibitions, they have a script that works and is very funny. That night, all the gags were forgotten. This was probably the most serious frame they had played against each other since that night in Sheffield thirty years ago.

It was a pretty turgid frame until Steve got in and cleared with a very impressive 57. England led overnight. When I got back to the bar almost all the players were in bed, even though they weren't playing until 1pm the next day. They had seen enough to know they didn't want to be the person who let their team down.

Dennis was pretty down: he hadn't played well today and his pride in performance was refreshing for me. Here was a guy with nothing to prove to anyone, yet it still mattered. I loved that.

The overnight frost made it a very fresh morning in Naas, I knew we had a long day ahead and I thought this one could go right to the wire. When the young table fitter Kieran asked me if we rigged the score to keep it close, you can imagine how that went down with Jimmy. In Thorburn's words, shots were being played like they were for pints of blood. This was more important than money.

Day 2 Session 3

ENGLAND 7 ALL IRELAND 5

Ali and Steve took the first frame of the session and 8-5 looked likely, but once again Ireland refused to lie down and Ken and Joe pinched the next frame. Then Joe nailed another re-spot and Ireland were back to 7-6.

Reanne was impressive in the next match, clearing with 54, the last black her trademark one-handed. I think it riled Fergal a bit: was she showboating? Maybe it was his way of motivating himself; it certainly worked, as his clearance in the next frame forced another black ball decider. Fergal stayed in the zone and duly potted the black again to get it back to 7-7. From now on in it was going to be singles.

In the interval Ken had to list his playing order for the final session. All of Team Ireland were locked away for a full ten minutes trying to outguess which way Jimmy would go. By this time Stephen Hendry had arrived to see his girlfriend Lauren who works on our shows and he couldn't believe how seriously they were all taking it.

First up was Ali against Dennis. It was closer than perhaps it should have been as Dennis came to the table 65 behind and made five reds and five blacks. Down to the yellow and Ali fluked it. JV said to the crowd, "Ali has had a bit of luck there." Ali quipped back, "I think I'm due a bit, don't you?" The crowd all applauded. Hard to argue with that one.

It was 8-7 – but many expected Fergal to beat Steve to make it 8-8, especially when the Irishman had a thirty point lead with just the colours left. Steve laid a great snooker, got the four-point foul and promptly cleared up. A critical frame pinched and it was 9-7. Fergal looked stern.

Captain Ken won the next match, defeating Jimmy, then Joe beat Reanne, her first singles defeat. Amazingly it was 9-9!

The session was overrunning so we had to delay the start time for the final matches by thirty minutes; good job as the place was heaving and we only had standing room in Goffs. Eight singles and eight points were on offer but we knew we'd be going to final black balls as neither team could get to the winning post of eighteen.

Day 2 Final Session

ENGLAND 9 **ALL IRELAND** 9

The reception the players got for the final session gave everyone goosebumps. Quite a few players said they had never heard anything like it. Just before Ken was called on I slipped him the Irish Tricolour. He draped it on his shoulders and the crowd took the roof off. I'd chosen 'Irish Rover' by the Pogues to bring the Irish team onto, and it worked perfectly.

It was like a pressure cooker in there. Almost every player not playing was either on the balcony or out in the crowd, save Steve Davis who watched from the players' room, glued to his iPad.

Jimmy played perhaps his best frame of the event to beat Ken, which put extra pressure on Fergal as it was his turn to play Reanne.

During the break in play he asked me if he had to kiss Reanne before the match started. I must have looked quizzically at him, but he explained that he was there to beat her not kiss her and be all friendly. That would be for afterwards. He was so in the zone the last thing he wanted to have was any friendly feelings for his opponent. It wasn't disrespectful in any way, it was just a statement of how bad he wanted to win.

That focus got him sixty ahead, but then he let Reanne in and she took all the balls to the brown, leaving her twenty-one behind with twenty-two on. She rattled the brown; it was sitting over the hole but in this atmosphere nothing was easy. I was really proud how our referees allowed the crowd to be supportive and loud but kept them quiet on the key shots. Fergal overcut the brown. He will claim it drifted, but either way Reanne pounced to clear up.

Everyone was stunned. England once more had a two-point lead!

There were only about twenty steps out of the arena back to the players' lounge but the way the players climbed those steps was fascinating. Those who had won were giving the high fives all the way, savouring every moment of victory with the crowd. If you lost you were scuttling up the stairs, shoulders hunched and head down, save Steve Davis of course... I had no idea if he had ever won or lost a frame – the Nugget, eh?

Being two points behind, Joe had a crucial match up with Ali. Again in a normal ranker you would make Joe only a 5/6-1 shot? But once again The Outlaw dug deep for his country and drew them back to 11-10. Steve Davis won the last of the session, again beating Dennis, so going into the final session it was 12-10 to England. With just four singles to play Ireland badly needed three of them.

Social media was buzzing. Ali tweeted: "Final Session tonight in the snooker legends in front of a packed house! So happy to be here with my health intact, love you all xxx"

Even then I had a funny feeling Ali would have a pivotal role in the outcome of this tournament.

On Twitter Mark Williams was demanding he captain a Welsh team to challenge. The world of snooker was getting involved in the event at Goffs, and more importantly for me, they were getting involved in a Snooker Legends event.

Ken beat Davis. 12-11 now, the fight-back was on... However it was to be the last singles frame England would win, with Reanne defeating Joe, Jimmy beating Dennis, and Ali clearing to win a tight one with Fergal.

Everyone took a breath. The climax I always plan for was about to happen. All eight players entered the arena. England needed to win three re-spots, Ireland needed seven, which was a big ask.

England took the first two black balls. Surely it was all over?

Then Ireland turned to the black ball specialist Dennis Taylor, and he duly delivered a cross double to keep Emerald Isle dreams alive. The noise inside Goffs was deafening; sure it was mostly Irish support, but it was impossible not to get caught up in it.

I stood alone behind the play. A smile broke out on my face: it was for moments like this that I had put in months and months of work.

Ken potted an almost impossible thin black to give Ireland one more point.

At 17-14 Jimmy turned to Ali. He knew just one pot would win the cup and how fitting would it be for the man who had battled lung cancer earlier this year, and won the biggest battle of all, to enjoy a moment of triumph on the table.

Fergal won the toss and put Ali in, the crowd went quiet... He attempted a full length double into the yellow pocket.

By the time the black hit the top cushion all of the England team had run across to judge the path of the black... and they began celebrating while it was more than three feet out.

Cancer survivor Ali Carter had potted the ball that saw England retain the Legends Cup. The final score 18-14.

The champagne corks popped too early, much to the relief of the table fitters who didn't want it all over the cloth, but no one minded.

I thanked a few people, especially JV, and pledged to return to Goffs again. This tussle deserved a rematch. Did I decide that on the spur of the moment in the emotion of it all? Of course not: I decided it when I saw the full house a few hours earlier. There is definitely money to be made in this venue with this type of event, especially if I bring The Rocket with me next time.

The party at the hotel went on until 5am – well, that's the time I departed from it. I'd like to report exactly what happened but Mr Carling has somewhat clouded my memories. I do recall everyone having a great time. Lots of laughter, even Fergal smiled. I think Reanne finally got that kiss too.

Before the event I'd had twelve posters mounted up with a commemorative plaque, a limited line of merchandise that we got all the players to sign. Joe Swail kept asking about them, as he wanted one for his snooker room. The truth is they sold out on the first day... all except the one I held back for him.

I presented it to him in the hotel after the event, and he was genuinely choked. I got a tricolour flag signed by all the team as well; I gave that to Fergal – a small thank you for selling a bucket load of tickets.

We were all battered. Dennis confided in me that on Saturday night he had decided to stop playing in these exhibitions as he felt he couldn't do the team justice. He was going to tell me after the event... then near on eight hundred people cheered and shouted for him, and it reminded him just how much he was loved. "I'll keep on getting the cue out for as long as you need me, Jason," he said.

Everyone loves Dennis; I think my girlfriend Michelle loves him more than she does me! Well, I haven't won the world title, have I?

The only other people in the bar that night were a wedding party. I think most of their album will end up being photobombed by the players. The bride and groom were deaf, as were most of their guests. As you may know Joe Swail is partially deaf, and at one point he staggered up and threw his arms round me and Dennis and said, "They're all deaf! I'm in my fucking element, it's a perfect night!" We all creased up.

Some players had early flights, most never went to bed. It was the perfect ending to the best ever event I had staged. My only regret was Michaela wasn't with us.

People talk about the atmosphere in the Crucible.

People talk about the atmosphere in Berlin.

Trust me on this...

There is nothing like the atmosphere created by a full house in Goffs, absolutely nothing. I can't wait to go back.

CHAPTER 24

The Future

In November 2014 the first snooker cue with a built in sighting aid was launched, alongside the first interactive training app. The claim is it will make you 'Play like a Champion' and change the way you play cue sports forever. Without my input, this cue would never have made it to a global market. It's called SightRight.

It's inevitable that because of my events, this cue and the subsequent training of SightRight coaches that I will continue to be involved in many aspects of cue sports for some time yet.

I now help manage Jimmy White, as close to a management role as he will ever need, and we've talked about setting up coaching academies in the Far East bearing his name.

I own a share in a snooker club, The Crucible, and that will continue to stage the successful Snooker Legends Pro Ams. I no longer have to scratch around for 10p pieces for light as I did as a child.

I also still have my involvement with Reanne and was so pleased when she got her chance at this year's World Championships. It annoyed me when people felt she was getting favourable treatment. The truth was the place was given by the WPBSA to the current world ladies snooker champion, not personally to Reanne herself. The reason behind this initiative is that the sport has designs about being recognised as an Olympic sport in 2020, and one of the considerations is that the game will need a properly structured men's, ladies and Paralympic tour. The immediate focus for Jason Ferguson is to get those other elements developed quickly.

Everyone within the game was aware of how good Reanne could be but the hype around her match with Ken Doherty showed what a huge commercial asset she can be. She should be around to carry the Ladies Tour for a few years yet but our focus is a top 64 place on the main tour... Watch this space.

One project that never happened was a documentary with Stephen Lee. Stephen was suspended for tournament snooker in October 2012 on match fixing charges. In September 2013, despite him claiming a lack of evidence and no criminal conviction, an independent panel found him guilty and he was given a twelve year ban, realistically ending his career.

I'd met Stephen a few times with Jimmy; he always proclaimed his innocence and said he wanted to have his say. We got on fine and he was very resilient – much more than I could have been having been through what he had. I thought a documentary similar to the one I completed with Tony Drago would make great viewing. I hadn't really studied his case, or the evidence around it, but I knew lots of snooker fans would be interested to hear his side of the story. We'd only heard World Snooker's side and it did seem right that he should have his say and then people could make their own judgement.

Originally he was up for it. We agreed the same revenue share model I'd done with Tony. He wanted an upfront payment but because of a misunderstanding over the sale of his cue to a fan overseas, Stephen also picked up a conviction for fraud, he got fined £1,815. Because of this, my partner at ROK then lost interest.

The only things I insisted on were that I would have editorial control over the finished programme and that Stephen would sit a polygraph test and answer every allegation around the details of the match fixing. I also made it clear that anyone he made claims against would have to be given the right to reply on camera to give the documentary balance.

Stephen flatly refused to do the polygraph test, claiming his family had been through enough. I thought it would have been a great way to proclaim his innocence, and also made great TV. I'm not sure why he refused to do it.

Stephen still wants to do a book. My own opinion is it will only ever happen if he vanity-publishes it himself. In the litigious world we live in I don't think any publishers would take that risk as even if Stephen tried to indemnify them it could still come back on them long term. He is angry, with scores to settle. Many will say he is innocent and there was no evidence; others will say he was caught, justice was served, and he got what he deserved.

I do feel very strongly that anyone who fixes a match does deserve a life ban from the sport, but I also think there needs to be consistency around all cases. One thing I do know is the game lost a player with one of the best cue actions ever to grace the baize.

Back to the future and occasionally I'll still play snooker myself – on a Monday night with the same bunch of lads I've played with for fifteen years. At forty-five years old I qualify for senior tournaments now as well, and yes, they remind me of that too. I'm not anything like the player I once was and that hurts. Age catches up with everyone.

I'm in business with Ronnie now with healthy coffee; who knows where that will take us both?

People always think that it must be great to be able to have a game with Jimmy or Ronnie but why on Earth would I do that? I already know how to re-spot balls.

Has creating Snooker Legends been a success? Maybe not always financially, but I've done pretty well and I've been lucky to work in a sport I love, one that I grew up playing. I didn't know that by taking my first steps at fourteen years old inside the Men's Institute in Mount Hawke that it would shape my professional career in such a way.

I am lucky, and I know what it means to have access to the stars of the game, and call them my friends, but make no mistake, I've worked bloody hard to get there... It's not easy carrying Ronnie's cue, you know!

Epilogue: Trolls

Late in 2013 snooker developed a social media problem. An anonymous Twitter account started up called Secret Snooker Player; they claimed to be a professional player on tour. Another one appeared called Jimmy the Wig, an account created to poke fun at Jimmy White.

For a while it was interesting to see some of the things coming out. Most of it was old news, but players were getting involved and a whole guessing game started. These trolls had very few followers but up until that Christmas everyone was playing detective and shortlisting suspects. Various names, and players, were banded about, but it seemed more like some random keyboard warrior craving interaction with a snooker star, rather than a snooker player himself.

The trigger for them to turn on me was when I named Reanne Evans in the England Legends Cup Team. I made a promise to name them, and so they started a campaign of abuse and false allegations against me personally, and Snooker Legends.

As everyone lost interest, the trolls started getting more and more abusive, like a child who craves attention. All the players were getting abused, my events were getting slaughtered, and I was being accused of ripping people off. I blocked all of them but that didn't stop them posting false allegations to the people who were following them and causing damage.

Early in 2014 I was accused of stealing the charity money from Jimmy's testimonial. Tweets went up saying I'd nicked money meant for Great Ormond

Street. At that point I contacted the police.

They were adamant that I should not interact, but also said there was no threat of life so it was a civil matter. The allegations made against me and my business would form a serious civil case against these individuals – but of course we had to catch them first.

So began a period of eleven months of silence, a period where a cork board at my home resembled something out of the detective programme *CSI*. These people thought they were being clever but they underestimated my resolve, and just like the police said, eventually their ego let them down.

Just by writing about them, it's giving them more oxygen than they deserve but I've known who they are for a few months now. However, everything has to be done properly so that when the prosecution comes I can make them accountable for every damaging, harassing and libellous tweet they've posted.

I have it all, and I will throw the full force of the law at them, as will many of the other people who have been libelled like Jimmy White, Stuart Bingham, Jason Ferguson and Barry Hearn.

Once this is made public, the people within snooker who provided information to these trolls will never play the game professionally again. They will deserve everything that is coming to them.

As Sylvester Stallone – Rocky himself – once said: "There is a natural law of Karma that vindictive people who go out of their way to hurt others will end up broke and alone."

As for me, as I said before, I now know exactly who you are... so just keep looking over your shoulder because I'm coming to get you.

www.snookerlegends.co.uk

@snookerlegends

www.facebook.com/SnookerLegends